Blogging
Second Edition

Digital Media and Society Series

Nancy Baym: *Personal Connections in the Digital Age*
Jean Burgess and Joshua Green: *YouTube*
Mark Deuze: *Media Work*
Charles Ess: *Digital Media Ethics, 2nd edition*
Alexander Halavais: *Search Engine Society*
Graeme Kirkpatrick: *Computer Games and the Social Imaginary*
Martin Hand: *Ubiquitous Photography*
Robert Hassan: *The Information Society*
Tim Jordan: *Hacking*
Leah A. Lievrouw: *Alternative and Activist New Media*
Rich Ling and Jonathan Donner: *Mobile Communication*
Donald Matheson and Stuart Allan: *Digital War Reporting*
Dhiraj Murthy: *Twitter*
Zizi A. Papacharissi: *A Private Sphere*
Jill Walker Rettberg: *Blogging, 2nd edition*
Patrik Wikström: *The Music Industry, 2nd edition*

Blogging
Second edition

JILL WALKER RETTBERG

polity

First edition published in 2008 by Polity Press
This second edition first published in 2014 by Polity Press

Polity Press
65 Bridge Street
Cambridge CB2 1UR, UK

Polity Press
350 Main Street
Malden, MA 02148, USA

ISBN-13: 978-0-7456-6364-7
ISBN-13: 978-0-7456-6365-4(pb)

A catalogue record for this book is available from the British Library.

Typeset in 10.25 on 13 pt FF Scala by
Servis Filmsetting Ltd, Stockport, Cheshire

The publisher has used its best endeavours to ensure that the URLs for external websites referred to in this book are correct and active at the time of going to press. However, the publisher has no responsibility for the websites and can make no guarantee that a site will remain live or that the content is or will remain appropriate.

Every effort has been made to trace all copyright holders, but if any have been inadvertently overlooked the publisher will be pleased to include any necessary credits in any subsequent reprint or edition.

For further information on Polity, visit our website: www.politybooks.com

Contents

Acknowledgements   vii
Introduction   1

1 What is a Blog?   5
   A brief history of weblogs   6
   How blogs have adapted to a social media
      ecosystem   14
   Three blogs   17
   Defining blogs   30

2 From Bards to Blogs   36
   Orality and literacy   37
   The introduction of print   41
   Print, blogging and reading   44
   Printed precedents of blogs   45
   The Late Age of Print   47
   A modern public sphere?   50
   Hypertext and computer lib   53
   Technological determinism or cultural shaping
      of technology?   57

3 Blogs, Communities and Networks   62
   Social network theory   66
   Distributed conversations   69
   Technology for distributed communities   72
   Facebook and Twitter as microblogs   76
   Publicly articulated relationships   82
   Colliding networks   83
   Emerging social networks   86

4   Citizen Journalists?   90
    Bloggers' perception of themselves   93
    When it matters whether a blogger is a journalist   94
    Objectivity, authority and credibility   97
    First-hand reports: blogging from a war zone   101
    First-hand reports: chance witnesses   104
    Bloggers as independent journalists and
        opinionists   107
    Gatewatching   108
    Symbiosis   112

5   Blogs as Narratives   115
    Goal-oriented narratives   116
    Ongoing and episodic narration   118
    Blogs as self-exploration   127
    Fictions or hoaxes? Kaycee Nicole and
        lonelygirl15   129

6   Blogging Brands   135
    The human voice   136
    Advertisements and sponsored posts on blogs   139
    Micropatronage   145
    Sponsored posts and pay-to-post   147
    Exploitation and alienation?   152
    Corporate blogs   155
    Engaging bloggers   161
    Corporate blogging gone wrong   164

7   The Future of Blogging   169
    Implicit participation and the perils of
        personalized media   170

    References   176
    Blogs Mentioned   186
    Index   189

Acknowledgements

Without the constant conversations with the readers of my blog and with other bloggers, and the inspiration of reading blogs throughout the blogosphere, this book wouldn't have existed. I love social media and am immensely grateful to those early bloggers and to the people who made the first blogging software, thereby opening up a new field – and to the visionaries, dabblers and practitioners who came before them. A visit to Blogger.com made me aware, back in October 2000, that anyone, even I, could easily make a blog. That opened new worlds to me.

While writing this book, I had the support of my colleagues at the University of Bergen, particularly in Digital Culture, and I would like to thank everyone there for years of conversations and ideas. I also spent a month at the University of Western Australia, finishing the first edition of the book while a guest researcher at the Department of Communication Studies. Tama Leaver (of tamaleaver.net) was especially helpful during my stay in Perth, reading most of the chapters and making many valuable suggestions for additions and reorganizations. I also received useful comments from Ingeborg Kleppe at the Norwegian School of Economics and Business Administration.

Working on the second edition, I've been able to draw upon feedback from my own students and from others who have taught and read the book. Thank you for all the help you've given me!

My editor at Polity Press for the first edition of this book, Andrea Drugan, was an inspiration and support throughout the process of writing this book, from working out the synopsis to finishing the manuscript. Her feedback was always rapid and helpful. I've also appreciated the comments I've received from the reviewers, which have helped me to make many improvements to the manuscript. Working on the second edition, I've had excellent support from editors, copy-editors and proof-readers at Polity: thank you!

Thank you also to Rand Corporation for permission to reprint the diagram from Paul Baran's paper, and to Jason Kottke for permission to use a screenshot from his blog.

And of course, my deeply loving thanks to my family, especially to my wonderful children: my teenager whose own writing online is an inspiration to me and my two little ones born after the first edition of this book was published. First and last, thank you to my wonderful husband and colleague Scott Rettberg for suggesting great examples and discussing ideas along the way, for reading the manuscript several times and giving me very useful pointers, and for being a splendid partner in every way.

JWR

Introduction

Fifteen years ago, the word 'blog' didn't exist. Ten years later, mainstream media routinely used the word without bothering to explain it. Weblogs have become part of popular consciousness with a speed that is remarkable by any standard. What is this new form of communication that so suddenly entered our culture?

I began blogging in October 2000, when I was working on my PhD thesis, and I've been blogging ever since. Like most bloggers, I learnt about blogging by doing it. Blogging is as much about reading other blogs as about writing your own, and the best way to understand blogging is to immerse yourself in it. However, blogs are also a part of a larger context. They are part of the history of communication and literacy, and emblematic of a shift from uni-directional mass media to participatory media, where viewers and readers become creators of media. Blogs are also part of the history of literature and writing. A path can be traced from early autobiographical writing through diary writing and memoirs up to the confessional and personal diary-style blogs of today (Serfaty 2004). Blogs are part of the current changes in journalism and in marketing. They are part of the growth of social networks like Facebook and Twitter, which in their turn have roots in the social network theory put forward by sociologists in the 1960s and 1970s, as well as in the network structure of the internet, which was designed around the same period.

Blogs are founded upon the link, building connections between related issues. Blogs are themselves related to many different contexts and can be interpreted from many different disciplines: media studies, the history of technology, sociology, ethnology, literary studies, marketing, journalism and more. Furthermore, blogs can function as a lens with which to see how all these fields have developed up until today, and with which we can understand more about other related social media.

This is the second edition of *Blogging*, and it is updated and revised throughout. Blogs are still blogs, five years later, but they are part of a very different ecosystem today than when the first edition of this book came out. Today, social media are mainstream. The blog indexes and search engines of the middle of the last decade have all but disappeared and instead we use Facebook, Twitter and other sites to share links to blog posts and even to discuss them. A lot of the shorter posts we used to see on blogs have moved to other sites that make short updates very easy. And photographs and other images are a lot more central to blogs today than they were a few years ago, both in traditional blogs and in new forms of blogging services where images are the main content, such as Pinterest and Instagram. As I have revised the book, I have added discussions of these new tendencies. The history of weblogging is extended to the present, of course, and recent developments in the relationship between blogs and journalism and blogs and marketing are also included. The basic structure of the book remains the same, though, and I have deliberately kept most of the examples from the early years of blogging, both because they are an interesting part of the history of blogging and because they are as relevant in understanding blogging as an example from today would have been.

The first chapter of this book is an introduction to blogs, explaining how blogs work. We look at four blogs in detail that are representative of three different kinds of blog. I'll then discuss the defining characteristics of blogs and, finally, look at the history of blogging.

The next two chapters look at blogging from two broader yet different perspectives. Chapter 2 sees blogging in a historical context, and explores ways in which major cultural shifts, such as the introduction of print, the spread of literacy and our expanding access to the internet, connect to blogging. It also examines ways in which cultural theories of communication and writing relate to the practice of blogging. In chapter 3, we look at current research on blogs as social arenas, in particular discussing social network theory and considering how social networks like MySpace and Facebook relate to blogs.

The fourth, fifth and sixth chapters of the book deal with different kinds of blogs. Chapter 4 looks at the symbiosis between blogging and journalism. Chapter 5 considers blogs as narratives, and explores the characteristics of blog narratives both in terms of narrative structure and in terms of the uneasy relationships between fiction, self-representation and authenticity. Chapter 6 examines commercial blogging, looking at the ways in which blogs are being used in marketing and by businesses, as well as at the ways individuals are setting up blogs as small businesses and earning a living from advertising revenue.

Finally, chapter 7 offers speculations on the future of blogging. Blogging has very rapidly become a popular form of writing – will we still blog in twenty years' time, or will other ways of communicating have taken over by then? Will blogging continue to increase the general public's ability to speak back and to be heard? Will it be subsumed by mass media, or change into something else altogether? What are the perils and promises of blogging?

This book contains references to many blogs, as well as to conventional sources. Blogs that are discussed are not generally included in the main bibliography, but are listed separately at the end of the book, along with their URLs at the time of writing or, in the case of blogs that are no longer actively maintained, their URL at the time they were active. However, blogs are by nature an ephemeral form, and some will have changed URLs or shut down completely by the time you read this. If so, I would recommend trying to enter the URL into the Internet

Archive's Wayback Machine at http://archive.org. This will usually provide you with search results allowing you to view the blog as it appeared at regular intervals during the period when it was active.

This book aims to be like a blog in that it constantly links to – or refers to – actual examples of what blogs are doing and what bloggers are writing, as well as to more conventional sources such as scholarship on blogs and their context. Being a book, it can also draw upon the strengths of this slower, longer format by providing a context and a sustained discussion that would be difficult in the faster, more fragmentary medium of blogs. But although reading about blogs is valuable for those who wish to gain an overview and to think about the meaning of blogs in today's culture, anyone who really wants to understand blogs will need to start their own blog, and to read other blogs. It's easy. If you haven't already tried blogging, give it a go!

CHAPTER ONE

What is a Blog?

To really understand blogs, you need to read them over time. Following a blog is like getting to know someone, or like watching a television series. Because blogging is a cumulative process, most posts presuppose some knowledge of the history of the blog, and they fit into a larger story. There's a very different sense of rhythm and continuity when you follow a blog, or a group of blogs, over time, compared to simply reading a single post that you've found through a search engine or by following a link from another website. A blog consists of more than words and images. It cannot be read simply for its writing, but is the sum of writing, layout, connections and links and the pace of publication.

You probably already have some idea of what a blog is, but, if you're like most of us, your concept of "blog" may be skewed by the kinds of blogs that you have read or that you have read about in the media. This chapter will provide you with a definition of what a blog is, but, more importantly, I hope to give you a broad sense of what blogs can be.

In the first edition of this book, I included a section on how to set up your own blog. Five years later, I am still quite sure that you will understand blogs better if you try setting up your own blog, but I think it's easier to learn to do that from the internet than from a book. Go to one of the common blogging engines like Blogger.com or Wordpress.com, and follow their instructions. It's free and it's really very easy – you just click a few buttons, select a template to determine what your blog should look like and you'll be ready to publish your first post. I prefer the more open systems like Wordpress, which you can even install on your own server if you want total ownership, but a lot of people enjoy blogging on more limited services like Tumblr and Pinterest. Even Facebook is a kind of blogging. So as you read, please don't be afraid to dive in and try things for yourself.

This chapter starts off with a history of blogging to give us a sense of our surroundings. Next, I've chosen three kinds of blogs for us to look at and analyse: a personal, diary-style blog; a filter-style blog that combines expertise with a personal twist; and two topic-driven blogs: a political blog and a craft blog. After examining these blogs, I'll discuss some definitions of blogs and consider how well they suit our examples.

A brief history of weblogs

Weblogs are unequivocally a product of the Web, and their history can be said to have begun at the same time as the Web was born. The World Wide Web was invented by Tim Berners-Lee and first implemented at the end of 1990, when Berners-Lee finished building the tools necessary to publish and view the first website: a web server on which to host the website, a web browser with which to view it, and the site itself. At the time, Berners-Lee was a scientist at CERN, the well-known particle physics lab in Switzerland, and his project was not seen as particularly important. The internet had already existed for two decades and was used by scientists, programmers and people interested in new forms of communication. Before the Web, the internet ran a number of protocols, such as email, UseNet (discussion groups), IRC (a chat system) and Gopher (a way of browsing files on remote servers). Many people simply saw the World Wide Web as yet another protocol. Berners-Lee's prototype web browser was entirely text based, so web pages couldn't include images or other media as they do today, and web browsers were not available on most computer platforms. It wasn't until 1993 that the Web opened up to the general public with the release of Mosaic, the first widely available graphical web browser, and also the first web browser to allow embedded images. Previous browsers had displayed images in separate windows, not in the same window as the text.

Most early websites were imagined as finished products rather than the constantly updated blogs and social media we are familiar with today. In retrospect, personal home pages can be seen as a precursor to blogs, but they were envisioned as complete presentations of the user's interests, not as something that would change daily. Websites were, however, often published before their creators imagined them to be complete. 'Under construction' signs were a common sight on websites in the 1990s, often accompanied by an icon depicting a worker with a shovel, as on road signs, showing the tension between the desire for completion that we had inherited from print and the constant flux of the Web.

By 1994, some pioneers had started online diaries. One of the first diarists was Justin Hall, who still blogs today. If you look at the early pages on his website, *Justin's Links*, you'll see that his site then was very different from today's blogs, and provides a wonderful example of the shift from building ever-expanding, densely hypertextual websites to developing blogs that are not intended to ever be completed. Hall used the section of his site called Vita to tell the story of his life (*links.net/vita*). Some pages show links organized chronologically from his childhood to the present; others are organized thematically by family, by places he grew up and has travelled to, by school, and by people who've meant a lot to him. Once you click a link, you find yourself in a labyrinth of interlinked stories that keep leading you through parts of Hall's life, frequently circling back to certain key topics, such as his father's suicide when he was eight, or his fascination with the Web. In 1996, Hall began publishing diary entries (in a section of the site called Daze), but each entry still had the same rambling style as his autobiography. Hall didn't start using blogging software until 2003. Up until then, he hand-coded each entry.

When Justin Hall began publishing regular diary entries

in 1996, his site matched today's understanding of what a blog might be. However, at the time, the word 'weblog' didn't exist – or rather, the word existed but was used for a different purpose. The term 'Web log' was used in the early 1990s to refer to the log of visitors that a person who administers a Web server can see. A Web log showed the number of total hits a site had received, how many unique users had visited, how much data had been transferred and other information about the traffic to the site.

In December 1997, Jorn Barger proposed the term should be used differently (Blood 2000). Barger's site, *Robot Wisdom*, was (and still is) a frequently updated list of links to other websites Barger has visited and wants to recommend, and Barger used the word 'weblog' as part of the title of his site, *Robot Wisdom: A Weblog by Jorn Barger*. This, it seems, was the first usage of the word 'weblog' in this sense. *Robot Wisdom* was a very bare list of links, with little or no commentary on each link. This style is similar to that of the more widely read *Scripting News* in the early years. *Scripting News* is the weblog of Dave Winer and was launched in April 1997, several months before *Robot Wisdom*, and also consisted of links to websites the blogger had seen with very minimal commentary. Here are the first few lines of Winer's very first post, with the links underlined:

> Tuesday, April 01, 1997
> Linkbot, Big Brother.
> Barry Frankel says Web Ads are Intrusive and Wesley Felter replies.
> Check this out. Amazing!
> MacWEEK: Goodbye AppleLink. (A tear comes to my eye . . .)

Winer is still a prolific blogger, often writing several posts a day. The most obvious difference is that each post is longer, giving more context and presenting Winer's opinions on the topic at hand. He will also often include links to more different sources. Today, Winer uses links to build an argument, pulling ideas together from different websites and weaving links into miniature essays. Winer's 1997 posts are much closer to *Robot Wisdom*'s simple list of links, logging the websites visited in much the same manner as the history menu on your web browser.

Early bloggers hand-coded their sites, meaning that they had to create their blogs from scratch and edit raw HTML code or use a visual HTML editor like Dreamweaver each time they updated the blog. In late 1998 and throughout 1999, several free tools appeared that allowed bloggers to easily publish and update blogs and online diaries using templates and Web-based forms where posts could simply be typed straight in. Open Diary launched in October 1998, offering online diarists free hosting and an easy publishing solution. By January 1999, they hosted 2,500 diaries, all of them anonymous. In fact, Open Diary required that users be anonymous:

> The Open Diary is a totally anonymous diary community. We don't want to know who you are, and we don't want your readers to know who you are. Therefore, please do not include any information in your diary that would identify you. Such information includes full names, street addresses, phone numbers, and e-mail addresses that include your name in them (like JohnSmith@xyz.com).
>
> We do not allow any such information on this site, and if you enter it, it will be deleted. [. . .] Remember, there is a potential audience of 100 million people on the Internet who could read your diary, we would prefer (and we think you would also) if they didn't know who you are. (opendiary. com, 'The Rules', accessed at thearchive.org's archive for 25 January 1999)

Early weblogs differed from many online diaries in that they were generally written by people who used their full name, and, of course, in that they primarily consisted of comments on other websites and not of diary-like discussions of the writer's own life.

1999 also saw the launch of Pitas, the first free weblogging tool, followed by the release of Blogger in August of the same year. In her early essay on weblogs, Rebecca Blood argued that the actual posting interface of Blogger may have influenced the way weblogs developed in this period from being sparse lists of links, like Barger and Winer's early posts, to being more essayistic, including thoughts on issues not directly related to a specific website and links to other blogs that led to conversations between blogs (Blood 2000). When you posted to your Blogger blog in 1999, the interface provided a small box for you to type the post's title, and a larger box for you to type whatever you like. Other blogging systems, like that at the still popular community blog *Metafilter*, had and still have a more rigid system. At *Metafilter*, you fill out several boxes, each clearly labelled with instructions to the writer:

- Post Title. Keep it short and descriptive.
- Link URL. Web address of the site you're posting about.
- Link Text. These will be the first words of your post, and will be a clickable link to the web address you entered above.
- Description. The body of your post. Feel free to add links within your description, keep it one paragraph long if possible, line breaks will be stripped.

Recently, two extra boxes were added: an extended description and a box for tags. The original interface leads to a very specific form of post that is quite similar to the early style of Winer and Barger. For instance, in August 2007, one could read posts such as the following:

> The Icelandic coastline. A gallery of photos of the rugged, cold, and beautiful coast of Iceland.
> posted by Gamblor at 5:40 AM – 18 comments

> Time lapse animations of planets and satellites. See what an amateur digital astrophotographer could do a decade ago. This is what the animated gif was designed to do.
> posted by dkg at 6:43 AM – 20 comments

> Statetris is Tetris with European countries or American states as blocks.
> posted by goodnewsfortheinsane at 8:53 PM – 27 comments

As you can see, the posts match the constraints set up by the four boxes of *Metafilter*'s posting interface. There are exceptions, as it is possible to compose a post without using the initial link, but *Metafilter* is heavily dominated by brief, sparse posts linking to one or more interesting or unusual websites. The comments, however, can develop into lengthy debates, often involving scores, sometimes hundreds, of participants.

By the year 2000, Rebecca Blood wrote that the transition from the sparse lists of links, or filter-style weblogs, as she calls them, to the more essayistic form of blogging had largely taken place. She credits the free-form interface of blogging sites like Blogger with this shift:

> It is this free-form interface combined with absolute ease of use which has, in my opinion, done more to impel the shift from the filter-style weblog to journal-style blog than any other factor. And there has been a shift. Searching for a filter-style weblog by clicking through the thousands of weblogs listed at weblogs.com, the EatonWeb Portal, or Blogger Directory can be a Sisyphean task. (Blood 2000)

But not all early weblogs were sparse, minimal lists of links. An early blogger who wrote considerably more essayistic posts than Jorn Barger and Dave Winer was Peter Merholz, who was the first person to shorten the term 'weblog' to 'blog'. Merholz simply noted this in the sidebar to his blog in 1999: 'I've decided to pronounce the word "weblog" as wee'-blog. Or "blog" for short' (Blood 2000). Merholz's posts to his blog *PeterMe* have consistently been more essayistic than sparse, often discussing issues of usability and interface design, the field within which he works. Merholz still blogs today and has maintained this essayistic style.

Looking back, blogs like *Metafilter*, *Scripting News* and *Robot Wisdom* are very reminiscent of Twitter messages today, and perhaps also of Facebook status messages. On Twitter, users are limited to 140 characters in each of their posts, requiring extreme brevity and often somewhat contorted language to get a message across. Like *Metafilter*, Twitter and Facebook provide small boxes to write in and provide the user with prompts that guide what the boxes should be filled with. Facebook initially asked 'What are you doing right now?', later changing this to 'What's on your mind?' Twitter used to ask 'What are you doing?' but now simply explains 'Compose new tweet', although if you press the icon that brings up a new window to write a tweet, you are given the prompt 'What's happening?' Presumably, we have already learnt how to use Twitter, and no longer need such explicit prompts.

Another factor in the shift Blood identifies from a brief to an essayistic style of blogging is likely the merging of two previously fairly distinct genres. Early web diaries such as that of Justin Hall have little in common with the early weblogs of Jorn Barger or Dave Winer, or with the *Metafilter* of today. Carolyn Burke, who started her online diary in January 1995, wrote at the Online Diary History Project, 'I wanted everyone in the world to expose their inner lives to everyone else. Complete open honest people. What a great and ideal world would result' (Burke, n.d.). The early years of the web were characterized by utopianism and optimism: finally, everybody would be able to communicate freely. Blogger's slogan in 2000, 'Push-button publishing for the people', takes another tack on the matter – not shared intimacy, as with personal diaries online, but opening up publishing to regular people.

Once free, easy-to-use blogging systems like Blogger.com and others were established, blogging took off. By 2002, the *Oxford English Dictionary* was asking Peter Merholz for a print source for the word 'blog' so they could include it in their dictionary (peterme.com, 14 June 2002).

The blog search engine Technorati.com launched in 2002. The number of blogs it tracked grew rapidly, from a little over 100,000 in late 2003 to three million by July 2004. At this point, the total number of blogs was doubling every few months. Blog search engines like Technorati made the connections and conversations between blogs much more easily accessible to outsiders, and provided vast amounts of data about the blogosphere, as people had begun to call the global networks of blogs and the conversations taking place in them. Technorati began to release quarterly reports on 'The State of the Blogosphere', which were much cited and discussed and gave some of the largest-scale pictures of what blogs across the world were like. Technorati still exists today, but after indexing well over 100 million blogs in 2008 they have cut back to only one million blogs today, and have stopped indexing blogs in languages other than English. Technorati today still lists the one hundred most popular blogs (that it indexes) but is now more concerned with marketing and advertising across social media than with being a search engine for blogs. Their now-annual 'State of the Blogosphere' reports still contain interesting information about the blogs they track.

In 2004, the year that Technorati saw the number of blogs double every month, Merriam-Webster declared 'blog' to be the word of the year, reporting that 'blog' was the most searched-for word on their online dictionary that year. By then, the media were writing about blogs regularly and almost everybody seemed to have heard about them. But in a survey late that year, 62 per cent of internet users still said they didn't know what a blog was (Rainie 2005). No wonder they were trying to look the word up in a dictionary.

During the next few years, other personal publication platforms went mainstream, making our idea of what 'blogging' is more splintered but also showing the success of the basic idea of individuals freely being able to publish online. Twitter was founded in 2006, and by 2012 was one of the ten most-visited websites with more than half a billion active users. Facebook launched in 2004, at first only for students, but opening up to accept anybody as a member in late 2006. A few years later, it has more than a billion members. These figures are astounding in demonstrating the eagerness of humanity to communicate. In 2008, the term 'social media' was adopted and rapidly entered the mainstream as a broad category that describes online many-to-many communication. In many countries, a majority of the population has an account on Facebook or some other social media. While social media sites like Facebook, Twitter, YouTube and Pinterest are not usually referred to as blogs, they clearly have a lot in common with blogs. Twitter is sometimes referred to as 'micro-blogging', with reference to the brevity of each post, and as we have seen, Twitter is very similar to early blogs like *Scripting News* or *Metafilter*. Many people use YouTube to publish a video blog, or 'vlog', where they speak to the camera much as a conventional blogger types on the keyboard. Pinterest could be seen as a visual blog where people share and comment on images they find online. And Facebook is in many ways a closed blogging system, not unlike LiveJournal was with its complex privacy controls, friend lists and possibility of sharing (or posting) status messages, links, images and other content.

How blogs have adapted to a social media ecosystem

Blogs were social media years before the term was coined and, in many ways, blogs still form the backbone of social media. Far more people are on Facebook or another social media platform than there are bloggers, but much of what we do in social media is at root a form of blogging. In a post to *Jerz's Literacy Weblog* on 12 June 2012, Dennis Jerz borrows words from William Gibson, suggesting that blogs have 'evolved into birds', changed so they are barely recognizable, much as the dinosaurs did. But although a blogger in 2002 might not have predicted Pinterest or Twitter, it's unlikely they would have been particularly surprised to learn about them. The basic idea is the same: let everybody share their thoughts and discoveries online. As I see it, the major changes in the last decade have been a greatly increased centralization within each service, but many competing services; far more emphasis on images; briefer fragments to suit reading and sharing habits on mobile devices; and a fragmentation of conversations which now to a lesser extent take place in the blogs themselves and are instead spread across Twitter and Facebook.

First, new blogging services tend to be centralized and often advertisement-driven, rather than installed on the blogger's own server and controlled by the blogger. You can use Twitter or Facebook very much as you use a blog, but you cannot host your own Twitter or Facebook stream on an independent server; you have to use their server, their layout, and accept their ads. Tumblr.com is another example of a blogging site that only works if you accept being locked into their ecosystem.

Second, the increasing use of smartphones with integrated cameras and internet connectivity has affected the way blogs have evolved. The first shift here was to short messages and updates. Twitter's 140-character limit was specifically designed to be compatible with the 160 characters of an SMS on a phone (allowing some space for the Twitter handle of the sender) but as we increasingly access the internet on the go through our smartphones, the brevity of Twitter also perfectly matches the small screens of our mobile devices and the little bursts of time we use to access media on our mobiles, for instance while waiting for something or on public transport. Facebook's mobile client allows us to use Facebook similarly.

As the cameras in our smartphones have improved drastically, we're also seeing that photographs are becoming increasingly important in social media and blogs. Facebook gives and more space to images in its news feed, and services such as Instagram allow mobile photo sharing, complete with inbuilt filters that let us make our snapshots look like vintage polaroids or whatever we would like, turning the limitations of the phone camera into aesthetic qualities.

It's not just photographs that are increasingly popular: graphics and images in general are far more dominant in blogs and social media than in the early days of blogging. Greater bandwidth allowing faster download of images, better quality screens for viewing images, online image-editing tools that are high quality and free, and the growing use of handheld devices and tablets for reading web content all contribute to the image density of social media today. On Facebook and blogs, we see that slogans, jokes and motivational quotes spread quickly from user to user if superimposed on a photograph that contrasts, illustrates or complements the written text. Infographics and visualizations abound, and with their colourful and sometimes interactive charts and diagrams they are far more appealing to a drive-by audience than is a mass of text.

Sharing links to sites that interest us is an important feature of social media, and this too has become more visual. While text-based sites like *Metafilter* still exist, sites that are shared on Facebook are now automatically displayed with a thumbnail image, and social bookmarking sites like Pinterest emphasize the visual aspects of a site, displaying images linked to websites much as a mood board with photos cut from magazines pinned all over it. Blogs likewise feature images more prominently than in the early years, with many standard blog layout templates requiring a featured image for each post and many blog genres tending towards heavy use of photographs throughout each post.

It is impossible to estimate how many blogs there are in the world. There is no central registry for blogs. In 2012, the popular blogging host Wordpress.com stated that it alone hosted over 50 million blogs, with more than 100,000 new blogs set up each day – but it did not state how many of these are actively being updated.

One problem with trying to count blogs is the number of inactive blogs. Many people will try to create a blog to see how it works, but then abandon the blog after a single post, or maybe after a week or two. The reverse problem occurs with spam blogs, blogs that are created by marketers and spammers that are simply foils for search engines, full of garbled, machine-generated posts that link to websites that the spammers want search engines to see as popular. Another reason it's hard to track blogs accurately is that the internet is distributed and there is no central counting house for blogs.

The media monitoring company NM Incite tracked 181 million blogs at the end of 2011, according to a post in their blog, *The Social Marketer*, on 8 March 2012. They do not specify whether this is a global figure or English-language only. The China Internet Network Information Center reported there were more than 300 million 'blogs and personal spaces' in China in 2011 (CNNIC 2011).

A better way of estimating the spread of blogging is to survey a representative sample of the population, or of internet users, and ask whether or not they contribute to blogs and read blogs. The World Internet Project collects data from twenty different countries and has found a lot of variance in the popularity of blogging across these countries. For instance, as many as 20% of users in the United Arab Emirates work on a blog at least once a week, but only 5% in Australia do the same. And while 95% of New Zealanders and 94% of Swedes *never* work on a blog, only 62% of Mexicans and 61% of people in Cyprus never blog (USC Annenberg School Center for the Digital Future 2012).

Three blogs

An immense range of different blogs can be created by using simple blogging software. We'll look at blogs that represent three main styles of blogging: personal or diary-style blogging; filter blogging; and topic-driven blogging.

Personal blogs: Dooce.com
Heather B. Armstrong, also known by her pseudonym 'Dooce', rose to notoriety as one of the first bloggers to be fired from her job because of things she had written on her blog. In fact, the term 'to be dooced' is listed in UrbanDictionary.com as meaning 'To be fired from your job because of the contents of your weblog'. Armstrong used this momentum to build a strong and committed readership for her still very popular personal blog, *Dooce.com*. Over the course of more than a decade

of blogging, Armstrong has written about working in the tech industry, about her relationship to her Mormon family, about being a mother of small children, about post-partum depression, about her divorce and about many other topics. Her style is witty and often sarcastic, and her blog includes a lot of photographs, often of her dog or her daughter.

The basic layout of *Dooce.com* has remained fairly stable for the last few years, but the colour scheme and banner image across the top of the screen are regularly changed. Dooce is, after all, a designer. If you're interested in seeing the changes in her blog over the years, you can look at the archived versions at *The Internet Archive* (archive.org). The blog has always maintained a large central area for the main content of the site, the posts. There is a simple navigation bar across the top with icons linked to her photos, and ads in narrow columns on the left- and right-hand sides.

Some years ago, most blogs had a small section in an upper corner that explained who the blogger was or what the blog was about, and many blogs still have this. Increasingly, though, you have to look for an 'About' link to find this information, and Armstrong has also removed her description from the front page where it used to be. Sometimes there'll be a photograph of the blogger as well, and often a link to an 'About' page. Most blog templates have these features built in, and they will often fetch this information from the blogger's profile or from a form that the blogger fills out. In Armstrong's 'About' page, she writes briefly about being fired:

> I started this Web site in February 2001. A year later I was fired from my job for this Web site because I had written stories that included people in my workplace. My advice to you is BE YE NOT SO STUPID. Never write about work on the Internet unless your boss knows and sanctions the fact that YOU ARE WRITING ABOUT WORK ON THE INTERNET.

Armstrong has done very well for herself after being fired. Reading the blog entries that led up to her being fired (they're all still online), it's clear that she hated her job as a web designer in a dot com start-up. Today, she runs her own web design business, looks after her daughter and makes a reasonable income from ads on her very popular blog.

In the first years of blogging, there were no ads. Dooce's blog shows the path towards the commercialization – or as many bloggers say, the monetization – of blogging. She introduced text ads, like the ones seen in her blog's right-hand column, in 2004, and graphical ads, like the large ad on the left, in 2005. By 2006, Dooce and her husband reported that 'The monthly checks [from the advertisers] add up to a comfortable enough middle class to upper-middle class income' (*Salt Lake Tribune*, 14 October 2006). I discuss how she transitioned her blog into a business more in chapter 6, 'Blogging Brands'.

Armstrong's primary subject is her life. Her blog is a diary that is open to the public. Of course, Armstrong doesn't blog everything that happens to her – this is not a secret diary but a diary deliberately written to be shared. Posts are written with care and wit, and are clearly edited before they are published. Some of her posts are short and sweet, like this small tribute to her eldest daughter, posted with a photograph on 2 October 2012:

> First born
> She gets herself dressed, makes her own breakfast, packs her own bag. She can write paragraphs of dialogue and read hundreds of pages a week. She shows her little sister how to dress her dolls. She's memorized a concerto on the piano.
> Somewhere, somehow in the last eight years I raised a human being.

Others share anecdotes about kids and the annoyances of parenthood, or chance encounters in airports, such as the 27 April 2011 post this is excerpted from:

> Then he called out my name, and when I focused on his face I did not recognize him. So I thought, hmm, maybe he knows me from my website? Maybe he follows me on Twitter? Maybe I slept with him and don't remember?

And then time did that weird, dizzying thing that causes all the noise in the room to sound like a giant fart underwater. Because then it came to me: OH MY GOD YOU BROKE MY HEART EIGHTEEN YEARS AGO YOU BASTARD.

He did. He broke it right in half, and I did not get over it for a long time. But that was when I was unmedicated, so I did not get over a lot of things including the rapid decline of New Kids on the Block.

Most bloggers who use their blogs as personal diaries do so less publicly than Armstrong. Often diarists belong to web rings linking diaries together, or they write on social sites like LiveJournal where they can set up friend lists and share sections of their diaries with specified friends or groups of friends. In these cases, the blog is often only meant as a way of communicating with close friends. Armstrong's posts don't document every aspect of her life as a private diary might. Instead, they present slices of her life, episodes and anecdotes that give readers a strong feeling of knowing the blogger, but that also keep many secrets. This is the aspect of blogging that Viviane Serfaty refers to as the veil of the screen (Serfaty 2004: 13–14). She argues that online diarists and bloggers use their writing as a mirror that allows them to see themselves more clearly and to construct themselves as subjects in a digital society, but also as a veil that will always conceal much of their lives from their readers. We'll return to the ways bloggers both reveal and hide their lives from their readers in chapter 5.

Filter blogs: kottke.org
Unlike diary-style blogs, filter blogs don't log the blogger's offline life but record his or her experiences and finds on the Web. Jorn Barger's *Robot Wisdom* was one of the first examples of a filter blog, being simply a list of links with no commentary. Most weblogs do however provide some commentary in addition to simply linking. Today's filter blogs range from the popular *Boing Boing*, which provides news on bizarre web finds, to *Metafilter*, a group blog where members post links

to interesting websites, to personal sites like Rebecca Blood's *Rebecca's Pocket* or Jason Kottke's *kottke.org*. While personal blogs like *Dooce.com* focus mostly on the life of the blogger, filter blogs filter the web from the blogger's own point of view. There are often dominant topics, but these may shift as the blogger's interests change over time.

Jason Kottke is a web designer who has been blogging since 1998 at the URL *kottke.org*. His blog is known for its witty commentary and expert opinions on the cultural sides of web development, design and new technology, and Kottke succeeds in combining his discussion of web news with a personal tone and the occasional personal story. The screenshot reproduced here (Figure 1.1) shows an excellent example of this. When it was taken, Kottke and his wife (Meg Hourihan, who coincidentally was a co-founder of Blogger.com) had recently become parents for the first time. Kottke's blogging had therefore dropped to a minimum, but when he did post, it was to compare his newborn son's reflexes to the motion-sensitivity of two recently released technological toys: the iPhone and the Wii game console's remote. After considering the various advantages and drawbacks of the iPhone and the Wiimote, he concludes that the baby is the winner:

> Newborns, however, are born with something called the Moro reflex. When infants feel themselves fall backwards, they startle and throw their arms out to the sides, as illustrated in this video. Even fast asleep they will do this, often waking up in the process. So while the Wiimote's accelerometer may be more sensitive, the psychological pressure exerted on the parent while lowering a sleeping baby slowly and smoothly enough so as not to wake them with the Moro reflex and thereby squandering 40 minutes of walking-the-baby-to-sleep time is beyond intense and so much greater than any stress one might feel serving for the match in tennis or getting that final strike in bowling.

In this cited portion, Kottke links out to information on newborn babies' 'accelerometer'; earlier in the post, he linked to

Figure 1.1 A screenshot of Jason Kottke's blog, *kottke.org* (taken 2 August 2007).

information on the accelerometers built into the iPhone and the Wiimote. He does include a touch of a diary-style story about being a new parent, but its style is very different from Dooce's, woven into a discussion of recent technology.

Kottke's blog layout in 2007 (see Figure 1.1) shows his enthusiasm for and knowledge about the Web by integrating 'widgets', pieces of code that you can paste into your blog template to automatically display your activity on another site. In 2012, the layout has been simplified and, as with many contemporary blogs, there is more white space and less information in the side column. As on *Dooce.com*, there is no general description of the blog on the front page, but there is a link to 'About + contact'. Instead of the 2007 widget displaying recent Twitter posts, the 2012 layout simply links to the official *kottke.org* Twitter feed.

Jason Kottke usually does not permit comments on his posts, presumably because of the extremely high number of comments he used to receive, making it very work-intensive to moderate comments and participate in discussions. From 2007 to 2009, some readers ran a website of their own called *KottkeKomments*, which pulled in posts from *kottke.org*'s RSS feed and republished them, the main difference being that comments were open on each post. In practice, the site was more a statement than an actual community. There were no links from *kottke.org* to *KottkeKomments*, so it was hard for readers to find the site, and only a small number of readers participate in the discussions held there. Jason Kottke does participate in conversations between blogs by linking to blogs in some of his posts, and he often acknowledges that he has found an interesting link or story in another blog by adding a line at the end of a post, for instance: 'via <u>Matt</u>', where the word Matt is linked to Matt's post at his blog *A Whole Lot of Nothing*. Kottke doesn't have a blogroll, but includes a list of links to 'sites I've enjoyed recently' in the right-hand column of his blog, and there are several blogs among these. Unlike many other popular blogs, Kottke merely gestures towards newer social media. The blog does prominently display a link to Twitter, Tumblr and Facebook accounts, but these only re-post blog posts, just as the RSS feed does. Kottke does not engage in conversation in any of these places. However, Jason Kottke does have personal accounts, and @jkottke on Twitter is fairly active, engages in conversations and, as evidence of the level of his blog's popularity, has over 170,000 followers.

Topic-driven blogs: Daily Kos *and* The Artful Parent

Jason Kottke and Heather Armstrong blog about issues that interest them. They don't limit their blogging to a pre-defined topic, although their interests are reasonably stable. Kottke is a graphic designer who mainly works with the Web and so most of his posts are about the Web, design or information architecture. While Armstrong was in the tech industry, she wrote about work and living in Los Angeles, whereas now her focus is largely on life as a mother of young children. Despite changes in their lives, their individual voices are constant reminders that these blogs are personal.

Many blogs are not primarily focused on the various interests of the individual blogger, but are instead focused on topics as diverse as knitting (*Brooklyn Tweed*), personal finances (*Get Rich Slowly*), crafting with children (*The Artful Parent*), data visualization (*Flowing Data*), politicians' use of the Web (*techPresident*), quantum theory (*The Quantum Pontiff*) or personal productivity (*Zen Habits*). All these topic-centred blogs share newly discovered ideas and information with their readers, usually providing links to more information. Thus they provide a filter to the vast amounts of news, information and conversations on the Web. While many of these blogs are run by individuals, topic-driven blogs are also often run collaboratively by a group of contributors. Often such blogs prioritize debate, both between posters and between posters and commenters.

There are as many different kinds of topic-driven blogs as there are hobbies, passions and professions. One large group within topic-driven blogs is blogs about politics. According to Pew Internet Research's survey of bloggers in July 2006, around 11 per cent of all bloggers write primarily about politics. *Daily Kos*, a liberal blog founded by Markos Moulitsas in 2002, is one of the most popular political blogs. Moulitsas writes many posts himself, but most are written by a broad network of contributors, both established political figures and community members of the site. Each post is signed by its author, often using a pseudonym such as 'Kos' or 'teacherken', and pseudonyms are linked to the user's profile, which includes the user's real name, a short biography and links to their activity on the site.

Daily Kos has moved from a three-column layout in 2007 to a simpler, two-column layout today. In 2007, all ads were for politically compatible sites, but today the blog simply serves standard ads. There are many posts every day, and most posts comment on and link to news articles, statements by politicians and ongoing debates, often with quite extensive quotes and some further discussion. Posts tend to take a news article, a press release or another blog post as a starting point, show readers specific sections of the post, and criticize or add to the points made in the quotation. The posts link back to the source, allowing readers to read the entire article if they so wish. This form of blogging is discussion-oriented and can lead to extensive conversations across blogs. It is not at all confined to political blogs but may be most prolific in these blogs.

The Artful Parent is an example of quite a different topic-driven blog, and is written by parent and artist Jean Van't Hul. The topic is clearly defined: 'On *The Artful Parent* I share ideas, information, and inspiration to encourage you to enjoy and share art with the kids in your life (whether in your home or your classroom). I post several times a week on children's art, seasonal crafts, and family fun.' Unlike *The Daily Kos*, *The Artful Parent* is a single-authored blog, with a post published 3–5 times a week. Most posts describe an art activity Jean Van't Hul has tried out with her young children. The posts are illustrated with photos, include instructions and information about where to find materials, as well as little personal anecdotes. The blog started out as a hobby; a site where Van't Hul shared her passion for engaging children in creative art processes, but with time the blog has become increasingly professional, with sponsors, giveaways, carefully catalogued posts to make the archives more accessible and the sale of ebooks of art projects for each season. There are, of course, posts about all these activities, and there are also guest posts and interviews with other experts on children's art.

In contrast to what you would typically expect from a book

on the topic, Jean Van't Hul includes her personal experience of an art activity in her description. For instance, she starts a post describing body tracing like this:

> Why is body tracing *so* popular with little kids?! Maia just loves it. She loves it when I trace her body with chalk outside. And she loves it when I trace her body on paper inside. So today when I asked her if she wanted me to trace her body (inspired by Lucia's post on body art with her art group), she was super excited.

The rest of the post describes how they laid easel paper on the floor, shows photos of the process and links to supplies you might want to use to do the activity at home: oil pastels and tempera paints.

Crafts blogs are a region of the blogosphere that has grown heavily over the last few years. In some counts, crafts blogs dwarf political blogs, news blogs or tech blogs (De Maeyer 2010). In a visualization of the top 1,000 most popular blogs on Technorati in 2011, Hal Roberts of *Mediacloud*, the Berkman Center for Internet and Society at Harvard, mapped the blogs not simply according to the links between them but according to the most frequently used words. Roberts found that 'love' was the most frequently used word in the top 1,000 blogs, and identified the 'love' blogs as primarily crafts and lifestyle blogs. Apart from love, the tag cloud generated from the 'love' cluster shows a high frequency of words like family, Christmas, children, cute, décor, quilt, colour, tutorial, vintage, space, fabulous, giveaway (Roberts 2011).

Like *The Daily Kos*, many crafts blogs have large audiences and focus on a specific topic with its own clear rules and expectations. There are some different genre conventions, though. Where *The Daily Kos* responds to news reports and includes long quotations and often embeds the videos it is responding to, crafts blogs like *The Artful Parent* focus much more on an extensive use of photos, grounding posts in the physical world around them. Although much of the content appears apolitical, there are many serious debates in the 'love' blog cluster.

Topics that are regularly discussed include sustainable living, work–life balance and feminism, all matters that are important in society and perhaps are given too little attention by political blogs such as *The Daily Kos*. It is true that the feel-good atmosphere of many crafts blogs hinders more overtly political discussions, or even topics that will engender controversy. For instance, when on 20 August 2012 SouleMama wrote about how her whole family had come down with whooping cough, she apologetically pleaded with her readers not to discuss the pros and cons of vaccinations:

> I haven't been sure how this particular chapter of our lives was going to fit into the space of this here blog. Because, I hope you'll understand, this Mama is very tired, and a wee bit vulnerable, and most definitely not up for controversy or playing the role of mediator beyond that of my five littles at the moment (*which is my gentle but sincere way of asking that we skip the volatile topic of vaccines in the comments here today. Thank you so much!*).

She later closed comments, because of course a debate did follow. In an addendum to her original post, she refused to state whether or not she was for or against vaccinations, pointing out that the strain of whooping cough her family had caught was affecting vaccinated and unvaccinated alike. She reiterated her dislike of debate, requesting:

> That readers kindly refrain from discussing the politics of vaccination in the comments of this thread, as I think the conversation is not only volatile and not conducive to healthy, peaceful debate in this medium but most importantly, entirely unwelcome in this, my space. There are forums and places which welcome debate online that surely you can find. Please think of this space here as my living room in which we've all been asked to leave our politics at the door and enter into the room in kindness and in the hope of finding what connects us, rather than divides.

On the one hand, SouleMama's polite insistence that readers do not discuss controversial issues perfectly echoes the perhaps old-fashioned rule of etiquette not to discuss politics or religion in polite society. Polite society, of course, often meant situations where women were present – and while avoiding controversial issues may have allowed women greater harmony in their relationships, it also marginalized women's voices in politics.

Another way of looking at the avoidance of controversy is that these blogs are intended as a way of focusing on happiness, even bliss. There is even a book titled *Blogging for Bliss*:

> Blogging for bliss means many things to many bloggers, but in the end it's all about connecting, learning, and giving back by inspiring others. With just a few clicks of a mouse you can be transported into a creative and inspiring community where quilters can learn new techniques, moms can connect with other moms, and artists can share their creations and gain recognition. Creative blogs are wonderful and welcoming places, introducing countless avenues to express one's passions. (Frey 2009: 12)

A less charitable perspective is that of commercial interest. *Soulemama* has become an income source for Amanda Soule, just as *The Artful Parent* has become a source of income for Jean Van't Hul. Most popular crafts blogs have ads and sponsors that generate a direct income. In addition, many publish books in print or independently as ebooks; they run online stores or they sell their knitting patterns as downloads; they offer online photography or sewing classes or specially packaged video tutorials. If you're making a living off your blog, you don't want to offend half your customers.

Because bloggers tend to read and link to other blogs that are similar to their own, it is easy to develop a skewed view of what the 'typical' blogger might be like, and this has led to several false debates. For instance, a regularly occurring discussion in the blogosphere concerns the perceived lack of women bloggers. Surveys have shown that there is a fairly even gender balance. In 2003, Susan Herring and her research group found that 48 per cent of bloggers in their sample were women and 52 per cent were men. Blogs hosted on typical journalling sites like LiveJournal and DiaryLand were excluded from the sample, as were blogs that had not been updated in the last two weeks. The selection was taken from the random function of blo.gs, a blog tracking service (Herring et al. 2004). In 2006, using a somewhat different methodology, researchers from Pew Internet Research found that 46 per cent of bloggers were women and 54 per cent men (Lenhart and Fox 2006). Both surveys demonstrate that the idea of gender imbalance was a perception rather than based on objective data.

It has often been noted that male bloggers tend to link more to other men than they do to women bloggers. That means that for people who mostly read men's blogs, it might look as though there are 'no women bloggers', while the reality is that they are simply less visible within certain groups of blogs. Perhaps we tend to assume, too easily, that blogs form a continuous network in which they are all interconnected. Jodi Dean suggests that instead of talking about the 'blogosphere', which suggests a shared community, we should talk about 'blogipelago':

> The term 'blogosophere' tricks us into thinking community when we should be asking aout the kinds of links, networks, flows, and solidarities that blogs hinder and encourage. 'Blogipelago', like archipelago, reminds us of separateness, disconnection, and the immense effort it can take to move from one island or network to another. (Dean 2010: 38)

From the political 'blogipelago', *The Artful Parent* and *Soulemama* are all but invisible, and vice versa.

Herring argues that the reason for the impression that there are more male bloggers is the emphasis in the media on filter blogs, which Herring's survey found to be predominantly written by adult males. However, Herring's group found that only 13 per cent of all blogs are filter blogs or knowledge blogs, a category Herring defines as 'repositories of information and observations with a typically technological focus'. Forty per cent of journal- or diary-style bloggers are men, so this style of blogging is not dominated by women. The effect, however, of the media and the focus of scholarship on male-dominated filter blogs is, as Herring writes, that 'actual diversity (and hence evidence of the democratic nature of weblogs) is discursively minimized' (Herring et al. 2004).

Defining blogs

The word 'blog' is a contraction of the words 'web' and 'log'. Blogs have developed considerably since the word was first used about a website in 1997, but the basic sense of a blog being some kind of log, kept on the Web, remains. The word log is taken from nautical navigation, and originally referred to a chronological record of events during a sea journey: tracking speed, weather, course and so on. The name originally comes from the practice of measuring speed by throwing a log attached to a rope overboard and counting how many knots in the rope passed through a sailor's hands in thirty seconds. Readings from the log would then be entered into the logbook. Today, other information is also entered into the logbook. Weblogs have retained the chronological organization of the ship's logbook, although their content is less ordered and less systematic than a conventional logbook. The implicit transfer of the navigation metaphor to the Web is fitting, as people in the nineties tended to talk about navigating the Web.

The examples we've looked at so far have many things in common. Their basic layout is similar, with the page divided into two or three columns, where the largest column is for the main content, the posts, and the narrower columns are kept for links to other blogs, information about the blog or blogger, links within the blog and ads. Some are written by individuals and have very subjective, personal writing styles, while others are written by a group of contributors and have a more journalistic style, although posts are clearly opinionated and don't attempt to be neutral or objective.

There are blogs about acrobatics, cars, fashion, fatherhood, finances, gadgets, gardening, happiness, health, knitting, life, mathematics, motherhood, movies, pets, philosophy, photography, poetry, politics, personal productivity, religion, technology, travel, writing, and of course, blogging. If you're interested in any particular topic, you can probably find a blog – or a dozen blogs – about it. If not, you can easily start your own blog. But what do these very diverse websites have in common that allows us to call them all 'blogs'?

Genres may be defined by their form or their content. Comedies, for instance, are largely defined by their content and theme. M. H. Abrams's *A Glossary of Literary Terms* (Abrams 1993) defines a comedy as 'a work in which the materials are selected and managed primarily in order to interest, involve, and amuse us: the characters and their discomfitures engage our pleasurable attention rather than our profound concern, we are made to feel confident that no great disaster will occur, and usually the action turns out happily for the chief characters'. The sonnet, on the other hand, is an example of a genre that is defined by form alone. Abrams's definition reads thus: 'Sonnet. A lyric poem consisting of a single *stanza* of fourteen iambic pentameter lines linked by an intricate rhyme scheme.' There is, admittedly, later in the definition a discussion of the kinds of subject a sonnet typically addresses (sexual love was most common prior to John Donne, who introduced religious themes), but it is clear that the main defining quality of a sonnet is that it is constrained formally.

Blogs are far more diverse in their subject matter than either comedies or sonnets. On the other hand, blogs are easy to define formally, and, as we have seen in the examples discussed so far, blogs share similarities in layout and contain many of the same elements. The most obvious is the basic unit of the post, but there are many others, such as the time stamps, the post titles, the blogroll (which is growing less common), the 'About' page and so on. Most definitions of blogs rely primarily on the formal qualities of blogs. The Wikipedia entry for 'blog' begins, as of 18 September 2012, by stating that a blog is 'a discussion or informational site published on the World Wide Web and consisting of discrete entries ("posts") typically displayed in reverse chronological order (the most recent post appears first)'. This Wikipedia entry was begun on 1 November 2001, and has since been edited by hundreds of Wikipedia users, and, despite many minor adjustments over the years, we might assume that it represents a consensus opinion. The definition of 'weblog' that I wrote for the *Routledge Encyclopedia of Narrative Theory* begins in a similar manner by stating that a weblog is 'a frequently updated website consisting of dated entries arranged in reverse chronological order so the most recent post appears first' (Walker 2005).

These can be taken as minimal definitions of a blog – however, they are also so broad that they could include many forms of website that are not typically called blogs – company newsletters, for instance, or online newspapers. If we see blogs not as a genre but as a medium, that need not be a problem.

The difference between a medium and a genre has become blurred with the internet. It's easy enough to say that television is a medium and that soap operas, talk shows and sitcoms are genres. This differentiation is more difficult – and perhaps less useful – on the internet. Scholars have suggested that, rather than looking at the internet as a single medium, it makes more sense to consider different authoring software as providing different media (Ryan 2005). A game made in Flash is thus using a different medium, with different constraints and affordances, than a video edited in iMovie and uploaded to YouTube. In this sense of the word, blogs are a medium, not a genre. Just as an artist chooses to use oil paints rather than watercolour or a director chooses to work with cinema rather than television or theatre, a blogger has chosen to work within the set of constraints and affordances offered by blogging software.

Within the medium of blogs, you might then identify different genres and sub-genres, such as the diary-style blog, the filter blog and the topic-driven blog, and at the next level, the political blog or the craft blog. Each of these carries a set of elective limitations – for instance, the filter blog would probably not include photographs of the blogger's cat, and the personal blog would probably not include frequent links to newspaper articles about politics, or allow several posters. Of course, many blogs do cross genres, and as with every genre there are exceptions and crossovers.

Ultimately, whether or not you decide to define blogs as a medium or as a genre depends on your perspective. As Marie-Laure Ryan writes in her discussion of media and narrative for the *Routledge Encyclopedia of Narrative Theory*, the same thing might be seen as either a genre or a medium: 'Hypertext, for instance, is a genre if we view it as a type of text, but it is a (sub) medium if we regard it as an electronic tool for the organization of text' (Ryan 2005). We could say exactly the same thing of blogs. If we see blogs as a medium, then the formal definitions are sufficient. These are the material limitations of blogs. An online newspaper or company newsletter may well choose to use blogging software as a medium. However, if we see blogs as a genre, or, as Ryan puts it, as a 'type of text', then our definition should include mention of the typical style and content that lets us at a glance say 'that's not a blog' when we see an online newspaper.

The personal tone that we saw in Kottke's and Dooce's blogs is one of the characteristics often said to define blogs. Evan Williams, who with Meg Hourihan co-founded the company that created Blogger.com, names three characteristics that, to him, define blogging: frequency, brevity and personality (Turnball 2001). This triad refers to the familiar though not uncontroversial rules for good writing: clarity, brevity and sincerity, a triad Richard Lanham calls a 'venerable Stoic theory of language' (Lanham 1993: 228). Lanham argues that such rules for good writing belong to a world that revolves around goods and commodities, where words are derivative, simple references to the objects they refer to. In today's information society, on the other hand, 'words *are* the "goods"' (229), and striving to be 'clear, brief and sincere' makes no sense.

Be that as it may, Williams's alternative, 'frequency, brevity and personality', does describe the gist of blogging. The first two points describe formal qualities: blogs consist of frequent, relatively brief postings. The third is a question of style and context: blogs are personal. They are usually written by individuals and present an individual's subjective view of – or log of – the Web, their life or a particular topic. Even company blogs tend to be written by an individual or a small group of individuals, as we will see in chapter 6. Blogs are generally written in the first person.

In addition to being a first-person form of writing, blogs are social. Most blogs allow and encourage readers to leave comments, and almost all use links to sources and to other bloggers discussing similar topics. The social aspect of blogs is included in this definition of 'weblog' from the *Oxford English Dictionary*: 'A frequently updated website consisting of personal observations, excerpts from other sources, etc., typically run by a single person, and usually with hyperlinks to other sites; an online journal or diary.'

It's probably not possible to construct a watertight definition of 'blog' that once and for all enables us to classify any website as being either a blog or not a blog, but in most cases people have no trouble making such a distinction. One sure sign that a set of conventions for a genre have been established is the existence of parodies of the genre – and there are already many parodies of blogs. A well-known example is *The Dullest Blog in the World*, an anonymous blog with very short, very dull entries, such as this one from 7 June 2011, titled 'Sitting down': 'I was standing up. It occurred to me that a more comfortable posture would be preferable. I located a chair and sat down.' Beneath each post is the standard auto-generated list of links to the comments on the post, a permalink (permanent link) to the post, and, of course, the date and time stamp. The most remarkable thing about *The Dullest Blog in the World* is the sheer volume of comments each post attracts. Many posts have hundreds of comments, showing how fascinated people are with this simple parody.

CHAPTER TWO

From Bards to Blogs

Blogs are part of a fundamental shift in how we communicate. Not too long ago, our media culture was dominated by a small number of media producers that distributed their publications and broadcasts to large, relatively passive audiences. Today, newspapers and television stations are adapting to a new reality, where ordinary people create media and share their creations online. We have moved from a culture dominated by mass media, using one-to-many communication, to one where participatory media, using many-to-many communication, is becoming the norm.

Blogs tend to be understood in terms of how they are different to the mass media that dominated the twentieth century. This is especially true in the media's presentation of blogs, which repeatedly attempts to understand blogs as a (possibly flawed) form of journalism. Journalism is a profession with conventions that have evolved alongside the technology of mass publication and mass broadcasting and that are contingent on both this technology and on the commercial system of selling newspapers and broadcast media to both consumers and to advertisers. We'll return to the question of blogs and journalism in chapter 4.

If we step back a little further, and look at the larger picture of communication and publication through the ages, blogs make more sense than if we see them strictly from the point of view of mass media. Rather than simply being a form born in opposition to mass media, blogs have aspects in common with many other forms of communication during the last centuries.

The mass media are not a very old phenomenon. Before the

introduction of print, mass distribution was impossible. True, kings might hire scores of scribes to write out their instructions in many copies to be spread throughout the kingdom, but most books and written materials only existed in a limited number of copies. If you wanted to read a particular book, you would have to travel to the monastery or nobleman's library in which it was kept, and ask for permission to read it. As print became commonplace throughout the sixteenth century and onwards, a great shift occurred in our understanding of what literature and information was. When we learnt to record and broadcast sound, and later moving images, sounds and images became governed by the same logic of distribution and ownership as print had been.

This chapter traces the history of communication and publication as it relates to blogs. The histories of technological innovations such as writing, print and the Web are intertwined with philosophical understandings of the importance of communication, such as Plato's resistance to the written word, the different values assigned to dissemination and dialogue, ideas of the public sphere and, in our own century, the visionary ideas of how computers might change our culture. Towards the end of the chapter, I'll discuss how these cultural and technological aspects can be thought of as influencing each other, either seeing one as leading the way or seeing them as mutual participants in a process of co-construction.

Orality and literacy

There were at least two major shifts in communication prior to the advent of broadcast media and, more recently, the internet. First came the introduction of writing; later, the introduction of print and the subsequent ability to mass produce identical copies of a work. We often forget that writing is a technology in itself, even without the printing press or the computer. When writing was first introduced, it was met both with excitement and with a great deal of scepticism.

Looking back to the transition from orality to literacy – from a purely oral culture to one in which writing played an important part – can be useful in understanding the cultural meaning of blogging. Our transition from print to electronic media has been characterized by the scholar Walter Ong as a *secondary orality*, a return in some ways to a culture more like that of the Ancient Greeks than of the post-Gutenberg society (Ong 1982). By electronic media, Ong meant radio and television, not the internet, writing as he was before the internet was generally available to the public. Some aspects of blogging are certainly very similar to oral cultures: blogs are conversational and social, they are constantly changing and their tone tends to be less formal and closer to everyday speech than is the general tone of print writing.

Plato's dialogues, written in the first half of the fourth century BC, deal with precisely the transition from speech to writing as the privileged form of discourse. His dialogues are written descriptions of oral conversations between Socrates and various students, and so the arguments Plato makes are presented as belonging to Socrates, Plato's teacher. The dialogue *Phaedrus* takes writing itself as its main topic. You may have heard of one of Plato's objections to writing: it will destroy memory. People won't bother to memorize facts, speeches or stories if they can easily access them in writing. Another objection Plato makes to writing is far more relevant to blogging. Plato complains that a written text is basically unresponsive. If you ask a person what he means by what he just said, he will answer you. If you try to ask a text a question, however, it will 'preserve a solemn silence' (Plato 1999) and cannot defend itself. Even if a text is proven to be false, the words will stay the same, while a living person might not continue to make the same false claim.

With the internet, this is no longer true of writing. Blogs can be and frequently are edited, with corrections being made after a post's initial publication. Most blogs allow comments; this means that you *can* ask a question of these texts, and, quite probably, the text will respond – or rather, its writer, the blogger, will answer your question. If the blogger herself does not answer, other readers are likely to do so, either in the comments to the blog itself, or in their own blogs. In this sense, blogs appear to be closer to the reciprocity of oral communication that Plato appreciates than to the unresponsiveness of writing. Perhaps, then, blogs are part of the secondary orality that Walter Ong wrote of.

A third objection Plato raises against writing is the way in which writing allows words to be distributed without the writer's presence. Words should not be cast out indiscriminately, Plato argues; they should be like seeds planted carefully in a mind that is ready for them, and they should be nurtured through conversation, in dialogue. Spreading words indiscriminately is wasteful, and a serious scholar would not do so: 'Then he will not seriously incline to "write" his thoughts "in water" with pen and ink, sowing words which can neither speak for themselves nor teach the truth adequately to others' (Plato 1999). Plato writes himself, of course, rendering his argument ambiguous at best, but this objection to writing was persistent. Up until medieval times, courts of law held witnesses to be more reliable than documents such as contracts, thinking witnesses 'more credible than texts because they could be challenged and made to defend their statements, which texts could not' (Ong 1982: 96).

Plato wrote dialogues, and he praises dialogue as a form of communication that is more valuable than dissemination, such as writing or a public speech given to a large audience. In much writing on new media and the internet, the dialogic nature of the Web is similarly lauded. However, in his history of communication, John Durham Peters seeks to dispel the 'often uncritical celebration of dialogue', writing that '[d]ialogue is only one communicative script among many. The lament over the end of conversation and the call for refreshed dialogue alike miss the virtues inherent in nonreciprocal forms of action and culture' (Peters 1999: 35).

Peters sees Plato and Jesus as western culture's primordial spokesmen for dialogue and dissemination respectively. While Plato argues in *Phaedrus* that one who would share his ideas should do so in person and in a close dialogue, Jesus told the Parable of the Sower, who distributed his seed indiscriminately, spreading out a message to the masses:

> A farmer went out to sow his seed. As he was scattering the seed, some fell along the path, and the birds came and ate it up. Some fell on rocky places, where it did not have much soil. It sprang up quickly, because the soil was shallow. But when the sun came up, the plants were scorched, and they withered because they had no root. Other seed fell among thorns, which grew up and choked the plants. Still other seed fell on good soil, where it produced a crop – a hundred, sixty or thirty times what was sown. He who has ears, let him hear. (Matthew 13: 3–9)

As Peters points out, Plato argues for the exact opposite strategy, mocking the careless farmer who plants his seeds in unfitting soil:

> Would a husbandman, who is a man of sense, take the seeds, which he values and which he wishes to bear fruit, and in sober seriousness plant them during the heat of summer, in some garden of Adonis, that he may rejoice when he sees them in eight days appearing in beauty? At least he would do so, if at all, only for the sake of amusement and pastime. But when he is in earnest he sows in fitting soil, and practises husbandry, and is satisfied if in eight months the seeds which he has sown arrive at perfection. (Plato 1999)

Both these parables or stories are metaphors for the best way of sharing ideas. The Parable of the Sower proposes that you should spread your message as broadly as possible and accept that not everyone will understand or wish to engage with your ideas. This, Peters writes, is how *dissemination* works (note that the root of the word dissemination, *sem*, means seed). Even though many or maybe most seeds will be lost, the benefit will be great: 'But the one who received the seed that fell on good soil is the man who hears the word and understands it. He produces a crop, yielding a hundred, sixty or thirty times what was sown' (Matthew 13: 23). Mass media clearly follows this model – a television broadcast will be watched by only a small proportion of the people who could potentially tune in to it, but that small proportion may be sufficient for the producers. Advertisers and telemarketers routinely try to spread their message to as many people as possible, and are often more than happy if 1 per cent or even fewer of the recipients take up their offer.

Plato, on the other hand, argues that dissemination is wasteful, and that dialogue with worthy listeners and the careful tending of communication is the best way to spread your ideas. This idealization of dialogue has been particularly strong in modern ideas of pedagogy, where experts in the latter half of the twentieth century have moved away from previous ideas of education as a simple transferral of information (a kind of dissemination) and towards the idea that knowledge is constructed by the learner in dialogue and interaction with people and technologies. Dialogue has also been hailed as one of the key features of new media and especially of the internet.

Blogs are remarkable for combining aspects of both dialogue and dissemination. In a sense, they are as promiscuously sown as the seeds in the Parable of the Sower. Blogs are published on the internet and can be read by anybody – or nobody. On the other hand, a successful blog must be tended as a garden (Matrullo 2002). A reader can ask a question of a blog, by leaving a comment on the blog itself or by posting on her own blog, and very often the blogger will respond. Well-tended blogs are not at all like the writings of which Plato complains, 'if you ask them a question they preserve a solemn silence' (Plato 1999).

The introduction of print

'The print-made split between heart and head is the trauma that affects Europe from Machiavelli to the present,' Marshall

McLuhan wrote in *The Gutenberg Galaxy* (1962: 170). McLuhan wrote in aphorisms offering outrageously vivid ideas, but as Elizabeth Eisenstein, a later historian of the transition to print, has pointed out, a statement like that just quoted cannot be tested and is thus difficult to build upon (Eisenstein 1979: 129). Eisenstein and others have detailed many aspects inherent in the transition from a society where spoken discourse was the norm to one where silent reading and writing was a main form of communication, and, in fact, this detailed research largely upholds McLuhan's broad generalizations.

Eisenstein argues that the introduction of print was a major influence on the way western culture developed from the fifteenth century onwards. The printing press was first invented by the Chinese in the eleventh century, but was little used because of the enormous number of characters in the Chinese alphabet. Its European invention, which was apparently independent of the Chinese technology, is credited to Johannes Gutenberg around 1439. Previously, woodblock printing had been used; Gutenberg's important innovation was the use of movable type. By using individual letters, printers no longer had to carve out a whole page at a time, but could set type more flexibly and more easily make changes or corrections. Movable type was quicker and the results were more durable. Print did not immediately change books. It took fifty or a hundred years for print to become a more or less standardized process.

Eisenstein lists six features of print that caused changes in our culture:

1   Dissemination
2   Standardization
3   Reorganization
4   Data collection
5   Preservation
6   Amplification and reinforcement

The radical increase of *dissemination* is one of the most obvious features of print. While manuscripts were rare and costly objects, print allowed many identical copies of a text to be made. Instead of scholars travelling to a text, texts were spread throughout the world on a scale never before seen. When Eisenstein describes the 'ferment engendered by access to more books' (Eisenstein 1979: 74), it is easy to see the parallels with the radical increase in access to texts that has become possible with the Web.

One advantage of increased dissemination was that bringing texts together showed contradictions between them. For instance, having three different atlases side by side, it would become very obvious if a country were portrayed differently in the different maps. This led to a greater level of *standardization*. Additionally, errors were dealt with in a more systematic manner. A scribe might make an error when he copied a single book. But with print, any error was replicated in all the copies, as with the 'wicked bible' of 1631, where the printers forgot the word 'not', thus making the seventh commandment read 'Thou shalt commit adultery.' The unfortunate printers were fined 300 pounds, a lifetime's wages, and all but eleven copies of the book have since been destroyed. This kind of mistake led, among other things, to the publication of *errata*, lists of known errors, and with that, a willingness to try to find and minimize errors.

Print also led to the *reorganization* of texts, as new standards were developed. Tables of contents, indices and alphabetical organization were not common before print, and readers had to learn these skills that today are taken for granted. For instance, Eisenstein quotes a 1604 edition of an English dictionary as noting at the beginning that 'the reader must learne the alphabet, to wit: the order of the letters as they stand' (Eisenstein 1979: 89). Today we teach toddlers their ABCs.

The increased number of readers also led to radical improvements in *data collection*, Eisenstein's fourth item. An example of this is Ortelius's great atlas project, the *Theatrum orbis terrarum*, first published in 1570. Ortelius requested amendments and corrections to the maps presented in his atlas.

The *Theatrum* was frequently revised on the basis of feedback received from readers all around Europe, and was republished in at least twenty-eight editions before Ortelius's death in 1598. Eisenstein notes that this kind of large-scale conversation about a topic was simply not possible before print: 'After printing, large-scale data-collection [became] subject to new forms of feed-back which had not been possible in the age of scribes' (1979: 111).

Eisenstein's fifth point is *preservation*. Although we do still have some copies of medieval manuscripts, and even of a few older documents, even the most durable writing surfaces can be lost, become worn out or destroyed. If copied, there will almost always be some degree of textual drift because copyists always make small mistakes. Of course, printed documents don't last for ever either but, because they exist in a great many more copies, the likelihood of some copies surviving and perhaps being reprinted is far greater.

Finally, Eisenstein argues that print augments the *amplification and reinforcement* of ideas. This particularly shows itself in print culture's use and reuse of particular passages from ancient texts. We have very limited access to these scribal sources, but, with print, we tend to replicate the same parts again and again – for instance, Plato's arguments against writing, which you have probably heard before and which were replicated just a few pages ago.

Print, blogging and reading

Another deep way in which print influenced our culture in general and communication in particular is the increase in literacy that occurred with greater access to books. Today, new kinds of literacy are developing as the general population is acquiring new skills and the ability both to read and navigate the Web and to publish their own words, images, videos, blogs and other content. These new literacies have been called network literacy, multi-literacy, digital literacy and secondary literacy.

The spread of print went hand-in-hand with the spread of literacy, that is, with the ability to read and write. It's difficult to measure the level of literacy historically because some people could read but not write, while others could sign their name on a contract but not write anything else. However, estimates suggest that in most of Europe, only 20–30 per cent of the population were literate in the early seventeenth century, while 70–90 per cent were literate by the end of the eighteenth century (Chartier 2001: 125).

Up until the fifteenth century, reading generally meant reading aloud. Often a reader would read for an audience. Around this time, which you will have noticed also coincides with the introduction of print, more and more people were learning to read and they were learning to read *silently*. Silent reading, which we so take for granted today, had radical effects. With silent reading, reading changed from a communal to a personal act, and it has been argued that this new solitary relationship between an individual and a text was a significant reason for the development of the notion of a separation between private and public (Chartier 2001). The solitude of reading and writing is, perhaps, changing with blogs, which are more explicitly social forms of writing.

On the one hand, a movement away from speeches, which drew people together as they listened, to printed reports, which caused people to draw apart as they read, could be said to have led to major changes in community structures. On the other hand, the fact that people unknown to one another could now read the same text allowed for a new kind of impersonal connection between people. Today's niche communities online are in a sense a more fully evolved version of this.

Printed precedents of blogs

Print media have been dominated by mass publishing, by dissemination rather than dialogue, but print also allows small-scale and personal print publication. In the seventeenth century, pamphlets were the radical new form of communication, popular and widespread due to the combination of the printing press, higher literacy levels and the lifting of censorship. As a history of pamphlets published in 1715 states, a pamphlet, being 'of a small portable bulk, and of no great price, and of no great difficulty, seems adapted for every one's understanding, for every one's reading, for every one's buying capacity and ability' (Davies, quoted by Knights 2005: 224–5). Periodicals also became popular during this period. In Britain this was due, in part, to the lifting of government censorship of publications in 1695 (Knights 2005: 225). Like blogging, the spread of polemical printed publications led to more publication:

> [P]rint was a dialogic medium: published claim provoked printed counter-claim, vindication, denial, or agreement. Such a dialogue was easiest to sustain during periods of press freedom – either when the laws regulating the press had lapsed (1641, 1679, 1695) or when the law was ineffectually enforced. The dialogue was necessary because the best way to counteract print, it came to be recognized, was through print. The more controversial print there was, the more need there was to enter into print to engage with it. (Knights 2005: 235)

In the nineteenth century, authors we today know chiefly as novelists also edited and published their own personal newspapers. Alexandre Dumas directed and/or wrote for eleven newspapers – he was deeply engaged with the new technology of the modern press, introduced in France in the 1830s. Dumas' first newspaper was written solely by Dumas himself, and was called *Le Mois*, with a tag line that sounds so bloggish it must be in use by some blogger, somewhere: *jour par jour, heure par heure* ('day by day, hour by hour'). Dumas's intention was to write a daily chronicle of events.

In the twentieth century, print publication outside of large mass media institutions and advertising was aided by the technology of photocopying. Newsletters for schools, fanzines and photocopied annual family letters are all examples of small-scale, amateur publication. Some blogs serve the exact same purposes as these, and are primarily intended for small-scale distribution with little idea of the communication being two-way. Indeed, Michael Faris argues that 'zines, that is, amateur, independently produced magazines, are a direct ancestor of blogs (Faris 2007).

The greatest difference between a blog and a photocopied school newsletter, or an annual family letter photocopied and mailed to a hundred friends, is the potential audience and the increased potential for direct communication between audience members as well as via the central hub of the blog. Although most blogs are only read by a small group of people, some of the audience will be random. A blog may suddenly gain popularity by being linked from other sites. Photocopied newsletters or fanzines, on the other hand, can in theory be re-photocopied and occasionally become cult phenomena, but the process is far more labour-intensive and in most cases too slow to gather the momentum that causes fads to spread on the Web. So while, as Marshall McLuhan argued, 'print makes everyone a reader, and Xerox makes everyone a publisher' (McLuhan 1977: 178), photocopiers don't change authorship greatly. Bloggers, on the other hand, or at least savvy bloggers, are aware that their audience may be greater than they imagine, and they know that they cannot control who is reading. That presumably changes the way we write.

The Late Age of Print

We are living in the Late Age of Print, Jay David Bolter wrote more than two decades ago (Bolter 1991). In the second decade of the twenty-first century, we are well on our way out of the Age of Print, late or otherwise. Tom Pettitt has referred to the cultural period roughly between the introduction of print and the introduction of the Web as the Gutenberg parenthesis (Pettitt 2007). Pettitt calls the period dominated by print culture a parenthesis to emphasize that the mindset connected to print is temporary, and that, from a broad historical perspective, it only affected a relatively brief period.

Before the introduction of print, Pettitt argues, literature and art were seen as malleable, flexible and changing. A story would be performed again and again, told by a storyteller or enacted in a theatre. A song or a tune would have no owner, but be played in different ways by different people. With the introduction of print, we began to think of literature as something that could be fixed in time and space. A book became an autonomous unit, it became an original object that could belong to someone – an author or a publisher. This led, in time, to the Romantic idea of the author or artist as an original genius. Pettitt argues that different art forms entered the Gutenberg parenthesis at different points in time. Poetry, for instance, entered it early, with fixed versions of texts appearing as early as the fourteenth century, before print. Theatre was later, with Shakespeare a transitional figure. Shakespeare used other writers' narratives freely, but once a version of the play had been printed, it was seen as fixed, as an autonomous original. Blues music didn't enter the parenthesis until the 1950s, when the standards began to be recorded by specific artists, who thereafter 'owned' the song.

Print still holds strong as the culturally most respected medium. Print is the dominant medium used in schools, and reading of print literature is the only consumption of media that is seen as so culturally important that governments fund programmes to increase its use in the general population. In a 2004 report, 'Reading at Risk', the United States' National Endowment for the Arts mourned the decrease in the reading of print novels and poetry, citing these figures as symptoms of a general crisis: '[P]rint culture affords irreplaceable forms of focused attention and contemplation that make complex communications and insights possible. To lose such intellectual capability – and the many sorts of human continuity it allows – would constitute a vast cultural impoverishment' (National Endowment for the Arts 2004). This is a common idea: that print privileges 'focused attention' against broadcast media's channel surfing and the Web's hypertextuality with its link-following connectivity, and it is echoed in popular books such as Nicholas Carr's *The Shallows: What the Internet is Doing to Our Brains* (2010). The opposite argument can also be made. In his popular book *Everything Bad is Good for You*, Steven Johnson (2005) puts forth the argument that video games and television are actually giving us 'cognitive workouts' that teach the same kinds of skills as maths and chess. Television narratives involve far more complex storylines today than thirty years ago, while video games require constant problem solving. It is also worth noting that the most recent medium, the internet, is increasing the amount of reading and writing people engage in, a form of textual practice that is completely ignored by the 'Reading at Risk' report.

With every media shift there have been sceptical voices lamenting the loss of whatever characteristics the previously dominant medium was perceived as promoting. As discussed earlier in this chapter, Plato famously argued that writing had great disadvantages in comparison to oral dialogue.

Today the ascendancy of print is waning, and while print is still privileged by schools and the National Endowment for the Arts, it is no longer the dominant cultural medium. In the second half of the twentieth century radio and television moved in upon print's territory. In 2012, the US Department of Labor's Bureau of Labor Statistics reported that Americans over the age of 15 watch television for an average of 2.57 hours on weekdays and 3.19 hours on weekends. According to the same survey, Americans spend less than 20 minutes a day reading (American Bureau of Labor Statistics 2012, table 11).

In the last couple of decades, the internet and computers have become increasingly important, although use of the internet still lags behind television and radio use. When television was introduced we listened less to the radio and started watching soap operas on television instead of listening to them on the radio. But until the last couple of years, television watching has continued to increase, despite the rise of the internet. According to a Nielsen report discussed in the Media Decoder section of the *New York Times* on 6 May 2012, this trend is beginning to turn, with young people's television viewing now in decline. There is evidence that the internet does in fact displace traditional media, but that this happens fairly slowly (Ha and Fang 2012).

A modern public sphere?

The public sphere is a concept introduced by Jürgen Habermas to describe an ideal democratic space for rational debate among informed and engaged citizens, a space that would thus be an arena mediating between state and society (Habermas 1991). While the idea that such a public sphere has ever existed has often been criticized, the concept is as frequently invoked, and many scholars have discussed its relevance to the Web and to blogging (Poster 1997; O'Baoill 2004; Boeder 2005; Bahnisch 2006; Notaro 2006; Barlow 2008; el-Nawawy and Khamis 2011).

Habermas connects the establishment of a modern conception of private and public to the establishment of a liberal, capitalist society, where news became a commodity sold by merchants. This led to the eighteenth- and nineteenth-century cultures of open debate in newspapers and in the coffee shops of large European cities. The open debates that occur in such a public sphere are seen as necessary to a true democracy.

The decline of the public sphere has regularly been lamented. In 1986, Richard Sennett tied the decline to radio and television. To Sennett, the one-way, mass broadcasting of radio and television made reasoning and debate between individuals almost impossible: 'the very idea of public life has been put to an end. The media have vastly increased the store of knowledge social groups have about each other, but have rendered actual contact unnecessary' (Sennett 1986: 282).

Sennett admits that this is not solely the fault of radio

and television, writing that they merely fulfil 'those cultural impulses that formed over the whole of the last century and a half to withdraw from social interaction in order to know and feel more as a person' (282–3). He sees this tendency as having begun in nineteenth century theatres and concert halls, where a 'crowd silence' (283) was for the first time established as a norm. Radio and television, Sennett argues, intensify this: 'You've got to be silent to be spoken to . . . Passivity is the "logic" of this technology' (283).

Today, audiences are anything but passive. In countries with high access to the internet, most of the population is on Facebook and using other social media, sharing photos, links and thoughts. Our increased participation in media is not limited to the internet: a Norwegian survey found that 38 per cent of Norwegians have appeared on television (*Forskning.no*, 22 September 2006). Mainstream media publications pander to our eagerness to share our views. Newspapers have expanded the traditional letters to the editor columns to allow readers to comment on individual articles in their online editions, and often provide an infrastructure for online discussion boards and blogging. On their websites, print newspapers show ranked lists of the articles that readers have most frequently read, emailed, blogged or liked on Facebook. In television, phoning in has expanded into SMS TV, where talk shows, quiz shows and music shows all encourage viewers to send in SMSes that are either displayed on the screen for all viewers to see or that function as votes: which politician do you agree with? what's the answer to the quiz? which team member shall we vote out of the Big Brother house? which music video shall we play next? Viewers' activity in social media is also displayed on television for certain shows, such as CNN and Facebook's partnership during the 2012 US presidential elections, where CNN used Facebook to poll viewers on their responses to videos and displayed the results both on Facebook and on television.

As we saw, Plato distrusted the indiscriminate spread of

words. Jürgen Habermas recently expressed a similar concern about the internet:

> On the one hand, the communication shift from books and the printed press to the television and the Internet has brought about an unimagined broadening of the media sphere, and an unprecedented consolidation of communication networks. Intellectuals used to swim around in the public sphere like fish in water, but this environment has become ever more inclusive, while the exchange of ideas has become more intensive than ever. But on the other hand the intellectuals seem to be suffocating from the excess of this vitalising element, as if they were overdosing. The blessing seems to have become a curse. I see the reasons for that in the de-formalisation of the public sphere, and in the de-differentiation of the respective roles.
>
> Use of the Internet has both broadened and fragmented the contexts of communication. This is why the Internet can have a subversive effect on intellectual life in authoritarian regimes. But at the same time, the less formal, horizontal cross-linking of communication channels weakens the achievements of traditional media. This focuses the attention of an anonymous and dispersed public on select topics and information, allowing citizens to concentrate on the same critically filtered issues and journalistic pieces at any given time. The price we pay for the growth in egalitarianism offered by the Internet is the decentralised access to unedited stories. In this medium, contributions by intellectuals lose their power to create a focus. (Habermas 2006)

If we read blogs through the eyes of Plato and Habermas, it seems that the authority of blogs might not be tied simply to who can write them (anyone) but also to who can read them. If we have too many writers and readers, we might, to use Habermas's words, suffocate 'from the excess of this vitalising element'. In seventeenth- and eighteenth-century Britain, similar criticisms were made of the coffee houses Habermas lauded as the birthing place of the public sphere: 'the common people talk anything, for every carman and porter is now a statesman; and indeed the coffee houses are good for nothing else' (Sir Thomas Piper, quoted in Knights 2005: 251). Broad dissemination clearly worries many. Free dissemination means a lack of authority, and ultimately, a lack of control.

While Habermas's criticism may be read as a form of media panic similar to that expressed of earlier kinds of mass speech, there are other kinds of criticism of blogging as an open, democratic public space for debate.

Hypertext and computer lib

Hypertext, which blogs depend upon, is considerably older than the World Wide Web. The idea of hypertext is usually traced back to Vannevar Bush, science advisor to President Roosevelt during the Second World War. After the war was over, Bush wrote an influential essay titled 'As We May Think' (1945), which was published in the widely read journal *Atlantic Monthly*. In this article, Bush argued that science had helped humanity to advance in many fields, including medicine, construction and even warfare. However, science had not yet been used to help us *think* more efficiently. In particular, Bush noted the difficulty of accessing new information effectively. The problem, he wrote, was 'not so much that we publish unduly in view of the extent and variety of present-day interests, but rather that publication has been extended far beyond our present ability to make real use of the record'. Bush therefore proposed a new device that would help us store and access publications, and named this imagined device the memex:

> Consider a future device for individual use, which is a sort of mechanized private file and library. It needs a name, and, to coin one at random, 'memex' will do. A memex is a device in which an individual stores all his books, records, and communications, and which is mechanized so that it may be consulted with exceeding speed and flexibility. It is an enlarged intimate supplement to his memory. (Bush 1945)

Bush sketched a design for the memex that proposed having microfilm copies of books and other records built into a desk that would allow the reader to access two screens, each of which would project a page of a document. The controls on the desk would allow readers to make connections, or links, between documents, and to add notes. Bush even imagined a profession of 'trail-blazers', people who built trails of links through documents. If you were interested in a particular topic, you could not only purchase a book about the topic, you could purchase a trail that linked several different documents about the topic.

The memex has much in common with today's Web, and in particular with encyclopedic sites such as the Wikipedia. As Bush wrote, 'Wholly new forms of encyclopedias will appear, ready made with a mesh of associative trails running through them, ready to be dropped into the memex and there amplified' (Bush 1945). However, Bush only imagined the memex as a single-user machine. A memex-user would be able to buy or borrow another person's trails and load them into her own machine, but Bush did not imagine the Web with its networks of interconnected memexes. Although the memex was never built, many people who were later involved in the early development of hypertext read Bush's article and were inspired by it.

The actual word hypertext was coined in 1965 by Ted Nelson with the following words: 'Let me introduce the word "hypertext" to mean a body of written or pictorial material interconnected in such a complex way that it could not conveniently be presented or represented on paper' (Nelson 1965). At the time, Nelson was a sociology student, but he later became one of the chief visionaries of hypertext. In a later paper, Nelson is more specific in his definition of hypertext, defining it as a kind of hypermedia: '"Hypertext" means forms of writing which branch or perform on request; they are best presented on computer display screens . . . Discrete, or chunk style, hypertexts consist of separate pieces of text connected by links' (Nelson 1970; see also Wardrip-Fruin 2004 for further discussion of definitions of hypertext). Blogs are what Nelson called discrete, or chunk-style, hypertext, although blogs may certainly contain or be part of more complex forms of hypermedia.

At the same time as Nelson began to theorize hypertext, other researchers were developing early hypertext systems. Doug Engelbart's invention of the mouse and the graphical user interface in the 1960s was crucial in this development. Prior to this, all computing was command-line based, so that the user would type in a command and the computer would print a response to a screen or to paper. The technology of the graphical user interface took many years to reach homes. The first personal computers were not available until 1975, and were sold in kits that had to be put together by the owner. They had no screens, but a console of blinking lights. Most of today's computer users would probably not have recognized these computers as personal computers. The first home computer with a graphical user interface and a mouse was Apple's Lisa, which was released in 1982 and followed by the release of the far more popular Macintosh in 1984.

In 1974, before the first home computer was available, Ted Nelson self-published a book that became extremely influential: *Computer Lib/Dream Machines*. In this book, Nelson foresaw a world where everybody could publish and author hypertexts. Ted Nelson insisted that 'You must understand computers now!' and many of his ideas were very close to the Web we know today. Nelson named his imagined network Xanadu, after the place where the pleasure dome was built in Coleridge's poem 'Kubla Khan'. Xanadu was to have been a network similar to the internet in that it connected many distributed servers, and in that it would hold an ever-expanding amount of documents – the 'docuverse'. Unlike the Web, Xanadu had provisions for copyright and for versioning. It included plans for a system of micro-payments where citations are tracked. So if I embedded one of your YouTube videos in my blog, for instance, then readers of the blog would automatically be required to make a tiny payment to you every time they viewed the video. There would be no broken links – where you follow a link and get an error message because the website is no longer active – because every version of every document would have a permanent address and be archived for ever. Links would all be bi-directional, so my blog would automatically show you links to every other site that linked to it. In many ways, Xanadu had solutions to problems we're now seeing with the Web – but on the other hand, its complexity ensured that it was never fully realized. Tim Berners-Lee's World Wide Web, as we discussed in chapter 1, was simple and thus got started.

Visionaries like Ted Nelson, Vannevar Bush and Doug Engelbart have been important not only in the actual development of technology but in our ideas of what the internet should be. Although Xanadu was never realized, a large portion of the people who were involved in computers in the 1970s and 1980s read and were inspired by Nelson's writings. The utopias described in this early visionary work have a lot in common with some of the most enthusiastic discussions of blogs today. Yet Nelson realized that a technology like hypertext and communication through a network was not a simple innovation: 'Tomorrow's hypertext systems have immense political ramifications, and there are many struggles to come', Nelson warns (Literary Machines 3/19). As Stuart Moulthrop wrote:

> Xanadu would remove economic and social gatekeeping functions from the current owners of the means of text production (editors, publishers, managers of conglomerates). It would transfer control of cultural work to a broadly conceived population of culture workers: writers, artists, critics, "independent scholars," autodidacts, "generalists," fans, punks, cranks, hacks, hackers, and other non- or quasi-professionals. (Moulthrop 1991)

Perhaps if we had realized that was what Tim Berners-Lee was up to, the Web would not have had such a successful start.

Technological determinism or cultural shaping of technology?

It would be easy to assume that technology directly affects the social organization of media and communication. Television production studios and printing presses require skill and a lot of money to operate, so of course not everyone can have their own television station or run their own newspaper. Since the Web happens to allow far cheaper and less skill-intensive access to publication and distribution, it follows, so we could argue, that the social organization of communication changes in response.

The idea that technology determines social and cultural trends and patterns is known as *technological determinism*, and has often been criticized (Chandler 1996). Although it is clear that technology does affect the ways in which we live, technology does not appear out of a void and is itself shaped by cultural developments. This more moderate viewpoint has been referred to as *co-construction*, a term that emphasizes the mutual dependencies between technology and culture. It is also important to remember that many of the ways in which we use technology are neither necessary nor obvious. One of the best examples of this is the dominant use of radios in the twentieth century.

Radio technology, which was developed at the very end of the nineteenth century, was first used as a one-to-one form of communication, a tradition that continued with ham radio. However, most consumer radios were designed as dedicated receivers and cannot be used for transmitting, so for most people, radio is a one-way medium. Bertolt Brecht, the influential German playwright who aimed at creating theatre that would make people think critically rather than simply sit back and be entertained, wrote about the potential for a different kind of radio in 1932:

> [R]adio is one-sided when it should be two-. It is purely an apparatus for distribution, for mere sharing out. So here is

a positive suggestion: change this apparatus over from distribution to communication. The radio would be the finest
possible communication apparatus in public life, a vast network of pipes. That is to say, it would be if it knew how to
receive as well as to transmit, how to let the listener speak as
well as hear, how to bring him into a relationship instead of
isolating him. On this principle the radio should step out of
the supply business and organize its listeners as suppliers.
Any attempt by the radio to give a truly public character to
public occasions is a step in the right direction. (Brecht 1964)

Early radios were generally two-way: they could transmit as
well as receive. However, the technology of radio rapidly developed into a mass medium, where a small number of media
producers broadcast to a large, mostly passive audience. Ham
radio, where everybody is both a sender and a receiver, still
exists, but is clearly a marginal activity in which only a small
number of enthusiasts participate. Radios are also used for
two-way communication in various professional contexts,
such as between police officers, taxi drivers and pilots, but for
most people, radio is a one-way medium.

Brecht's comment shows that radio could have developed
differently. Ham radio could have been the dominant medium
to come out of the technology of radio transmission, and it
could have become what Brecht believed would be 'the finest
possible communication apparatus in public life'. Instead, it
remained a one-way medium.

Perhaps today's mobile phones, and especially smartphones,
are the implementation of Brecht's dream of two-way radio.
Radio talk shows do in fact 'organize . . . listeners as suppliers',
as Brecht wrote, combining telephone and radio technology
by having listeners call in to give their opinions. Telephones
without radio, however, primarily allow one-to-one communication and, while this can strengthen existing relationships, it
doesn't open up new possibilities. I like to imagine that what
Brecht was describing was peer-to-peer radio: podcasting.

So why wasn't radio used as a two-way medium? Why didn't

it 'let the listener speak as well as hear', and 'bring him into a relationship instead of isolating him'? Why was the twentieth-century media – not just radio, but newspapers, cinema and later television, so dominated by a one-to-many, mass media approach?

Part of the reason why uni-directional mass media dominated was simply cost: it costs a lot to set up a pre-digital printing press or a professional broadcasting studio, and with traditional technology, specialized technical skills were needed such as filming, editing and typography. A highly professionalized class of journalists and editors developed in parallel. This explanation takes technological limitations as the starting point, adding the issues of socio-economic status and access to money.

Technology was not the only reason, however: legislation limiting broadcasting rights to established players has had just as large an impact on the shaping of the media as has technology. To start a television station in the twentieth century, you didn't simply need skills and equipment – in many countries, you also needed a licence from the government to have a frequency allocated to your station. There is a technological side to this: the total number of frequencies that can be used for analogue television and radio broadcast is limited, so the choice to restrict the right to broadcast was a way of managing a scarce resource that was seen to belong to the public. The early years of radio broadcast in the United States were characterized by what Andrew Crisell calls 'aerial anarchy' (Crisell 2002: 18), but since the Communications Act of 1934, broadcast airwaves have been regulated by the Federal Communications Commission, known as the FCC (Epstein 1997). In many European countries, regulation was so strict that only a single state broadcaster was permitted to use the airwaves. The Norwegian broadcasting monopoly did not end until the 1980s (Bastiansen and Dahl 2003).

There have always been ways of avoiding these regulations. For instance, Radio Luxembourg broadcast in English from

Luxembourg on frequencies that were easily received on radios in the United Kingdom and other Western European countries, thus escaping the state monopolies in some of these countries. During the Second World War, radio was an important way for the resistance movement to communicate with the population. Other so-called 'pirate radio stations' have broadcast from ships outside of a country's waters or simply used frequencies they are not entitled to use. With the internet and digital distribution of audiovisual media, the scarcity that led to the regulation of broadcasting no longer exists: simply connect more servers to the network and there will be room for more communication.

[handwritten note in margin: but still there (some) is China, N. Korea]

Another, more culturally based, argument for why mass media were so dominant is that twentieth-century culture was fixed in the mindset of print, a mindset that is only around 400 years old. A major aspect of the print-based mindset is that cultural expression is something that is produced by an individual or a small group of people, and that, once produced, it is fixed – it doesn't change. Additionally, this product is a commodity that can be sold and that is owned by a person or company. We think of *Romeo and Juliet*, for instance, not simply as a love story about two teenagers, but as a specific text written by Shakespeare. Performances of the play are not seen as the original; they are enactments of the fixed text. Mass media follow this pattern in producing authoritative versions created by a small number of people and spread to large audiences. The exact copies of a television programme that are viewed by millions of people at exactly the same time are equivalent to the identical copies of printed books that are distributed to hundreds or millions of readers.

Blogs and the social publishing and communication forms that have developed on the Web are part of this larger picture of communication and publishing through the ages. They allow more dialogue than the pre-digital written word, and allow even cheaper and more extensive distribution than print or broadcasting. Blogs can be seen as belonging to the post-Gutenberg era, a time after the dominance of print and of mass media. They use technologies first imagined by visionaries of hypertext, but are more social than even these visionaries imagined. In the next chapter, we will focus on the social aspects of blogs and of social networking sites, a kind of communication very closely connected to blogs and that might even be seen as a kind of blogging.

CHAPTER THREE

Blogs, Communities and Networks

Blogs are social. Bloggers don't simply write to their 'Dear Diary', they write into the world with a clear expectation of having readers. That readership does not necessarily need to be very large. On the internet, everyone is famous to fifteen people, David Weinberger wrote, in a twist on Andy Warhol's familiar line about everyone getting their fifteen minutes of fame (Weinberger 2002: 104). Often, an audience of fifteen close friends, or of fifteen people who are genuinely interested in what you are writing about, is quite sufficient.

Instead of mass communication from a few producers to large, mostly passive audiences, blogs support a dense network of small audiences and many producers. Social media has become an everyday term referring to blogs and other online sites where users can share their own content. Although social media is a mainstream, very well-established term today, it is quite recent, and was not in current usage until 2008, just after the first edition of this book was published. Before that, the kinds of sites and media we call social media today were known as social software, or as social network sites. Even earlier, we talked about online communities or virtual communities, terms that included discussion boards and mailing lists but also online, multi-user games such as MUDs and MOOs or the MMOGs of the 2000s. The shift from *community* to *software* or *site* and to today's *media* is telling, and speaks of the different power constellations that have been able to define these spaces. The early online communities were almost entirely user run and were not commercial enterprises. In the years of social software, after the dot com

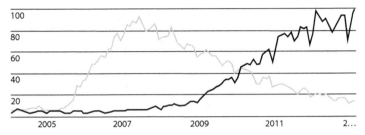

Figure 3.1 This Google Trends chart shows searches for 'Web 2.0' and searches for 'social media' from 2004 until early 2013. Google users searched for 'Web 2.0' frequently from 2006 but their searches sank after 2007. Searches for 'social media' began rising towards the end of 2008.

crash of the late 1990s, when technology was slowly being seen as profitable again, perhaps the platform and the system was central. We started calling it social media when the traditional media started paying attention and realizing that they needed to engage with this peer-to-peer publication.

It is difficult to pinpoint the origin of the term 'social media', but it is clear that it was used in a limited fashion well before 2008. Google Trends allows us to compare the frequency with which different terms were searched for on Google over time, and the chart generated when you ask it to compare 'social media' and 'Web 2.0' is very illustrative (see Figure 3.1).

Figure 3.1 shows how the term 'Web 2.0' increased greatly in popularity (or at least in search volume) from 2005 until 2007 and then began to sink. There are very few searches for 'social media' until the end of 2008, but searches for the term rise steadily after that. The term 'social media' has only recently become as frequently searched for as 'Web 2.0' was in its heyday, but that may simply be because it's a more self-explanatory term than 'Web 2.0', so that less people need to search for a definition. If you use the Google Trends tool (google.com/trends) to search news instead of search terms, you will see that the term 'Web 2.0' has relatively low usage in traditional news media, even when it was being searched for a lot by Google users. 'Social media', on the other hand, is used more and more in the news media from 2008 onwards. That would support my argument that one of the reasons 'social media' stuck as a term was that it made sense to traditional media outlets suddenly interested in and keenly aware of their dependence upon social media.

Blogs are a relatively free-form type of social media, and are decentralized, often running on their authors' own domains and connecting haphazardly to other blogs. Social media is often centralized on a single server, like Facebook, Tumblr or Pinterest, where all users have profiles on the same domain, and the system automatically links to the profiles of the people you've designated as friends. Some blogging sites are also centralized in this way, such as LiveJournal or blogs hosted on Wordpress.com or Blogspot.com. Like Facebook, these blogging sites will often allow bloggers to mark other bloggers as friends and may provide limited access to a blog to readers who are not the bloggers' friends. Even blogs that are not part of a centralized site like LiveJournal can, however, be seen as social media, and, though decentralized, blogs certainly map and perform a social network. Usually, this network is most visible through links. Many blogs have blogrolls that provide a list of other blogs that the blogger frequents. If the blog allows comments, commenters will generally leave links to their own blogs. Additionally, most blogs also link to conversations that are happening elsewhere in other blogs.

The links between blogs can be read by computers. Search engines and more specialized services use them to trace the patterns and connections between blogs. By tracking links from blogs, search engines like Google Blog can track trends. A few years ago, several different services tracked trends in blogs, including Technorati and Blogpulse. By indexing blogs and tracking what blogs linked to, services like these would show which YouTube videos or books, movies or news articles were generating the most buzz in the blogosphere. These external services provided an *exoskeleton* for blogs, displaying a community between blogs that is not necessarily immediately visible to a casual visitor.

A new blogger who doesn't already have connections to other bloggers may find it hard to enter this somewhat implicit social network. Other online communities, such as YouTube, Tumblr and Facebook, are gathered on a single site and can thus immediately provide new bloggers with suggestions as to where friends or potential connections might be. These sites can be said to provide an *intraskeleton* for the social network. Today, there is a lot less emphasis on tracking trends in blogs. Instead, the tendency is for larger, proprietary networks such as Facebook, Twitter or Wordpress.com to emphasize the 'trend-ing' articles, posts or topics in their own networks. Twitter does this explicitly in the list of 'Trends' shown on their homepage and next to a user's feed. Users can set their list of 'Trends' to be global or local to a country or large regional centre. On Facebook, the posts, links or images that have received the most likes and comments are pushed up to the top of your news feed. You will quite often see public items from people or pages you don't subscribe to if one or more of your friends has liked or commented on a popular post. Of course, you also get posts that are really just advertisements, and Facebook is continuously trying out new algorithms to achieve the perfect balance between content we actually want to see and content that will make them money. Wordpress.com and other blog-ging platforms also prominently display popular blog posts from their network on the front page. And many external sites, like newspapers or some blogs, use Facebook's 'open graph' to display their most popular posts, or at least those that are the most 'liked' on Facebook.

Much current research on blogs discusses them in relation to social media and social network sites. Additionally, many of the new ways blogs are being used are closely connected to other uses of social media where blogs form part but not the entirety of the site. Blogs are a form of social media that allows the individual to maintain power to a far greater extent than the most popular social media sites today. They shaped the vanguard of social media and are still a vital part of social media today. Blogs also inspire other genres within social media. Twitter, Pinterest, Facebook and Tumblr can all be described as blogs and maintain some of the key features of blogs: individual users can share text or images or other content with each other.

In this chapter, I will discuss some of these new ways blogs are evolving and present some important ideas from current research. But first let's look at the background that shapes current theories of social media.

Social network theory

A lot of the work on social software and social media builds upon sociological theories of social networks, such as the sociologist Mark Granovetter's theory of weak ties (1973). Granovetter was interested in how ideas spread through communities, and argued that *weak ties* between individuals are more important than *strong ties* for the broad dissemination of information. His argument is fairly simple (though backed by considerable data and analysis): if A and B know each other very well, and A and C also know each other very well, it is highly likely that B and C also know each other. If A needs a job, she'll ask B and C. They probably won't have any new information, because A already shares most of the information that B and C have. There's a far greater chance A will get new information – for instance, about a job that might suit her – from her weak ties, that is from acquaintances and people that she doesn't see very often. The greater social distance between A and her acquaintance D means that D knows more things that A doesn't already know.

Weak ties are also important because they work as bridges between social groups. People who are bridges between two groups may appear to be socially isolated but actually have weak ties with two or more groups, and these weak ties give them very early access to new information. Granovetter connects this to the 'small world' experiments conducted by Stanley Milgram and his associates (Milgram 1967) and replicated and expanded upon by many researchers since. The experiments are named for the common exclamation 'What a small world!' when people realize they both know the same person. In the experiments, Milgram's team asked participants to send a booklet to a randomly chosen target person by forwarding it to a person they knew who was more likely than themselves to know the target. Although many of the booklets never reached their target, and the project had significant problems, the booklets that did reach their goal had an average of six connections in the chain, leading to the popular idea of there being 'six degrees of connection' between any two people in the world. The original study dealt only with people within the United States, and the booklets had to be passed on in person rather than by mail. There are current studies trying to find out whether the phenomenon might exist globally, and in digital forms – how many forwards of an email does it take for the email to reach a specific person not known to the original recipient? Back in 1973, however, Granovetter noted that Milgram's studies found that the chain was more likely to be completed if there was a *weak tie* between people in the chain. That is, if a person passed on the booklet to an acquaintance rather than to a family member or close friend, there was a higher chance that it would reach its target, particularly in interracial chains.

In terms of social networks, links between blogs can signify that two bloggers know each other and think of each other as friends or acquaintances, but they may also simply signify that one blogger likes reading another blogger's posts. Social networks usually develop through family ties, a common job or a shared neighbourhood, rather than purely for information gathering. Blogs, on the other hand, may exist primarily as networks for sharing ideas, trends and information. Take fashion bloggers, for instance. Fashion bloggers, like Agathe

Bjørnsdatter at *Style Bytes*, post photos of their own outfits or of well-dressed people they've seen on the street. They might also share ideas, write about where you can buy certain garments or accessories, post notes and photos from fashion shows or magazines, and comment on trends. Most fashion blogs link to other fashion blogs, sensibly enough, both because the bloggers read these and because their readers are likely to be interested in them. So by looking at the links between fashion blogs, you can see a map of a social network or community of interest. This social network is primarily about the sharing of information. The network isn't exclusively about information, of course. Trust is built, as are friendships, alliances and controversies. Trends and styles spread and evolve within the network, not necessarily as something deliberate, but simply in the way certain conventions are likely to arise, in the length of posts, for instance, or in the use of photos, the style of writing or the number of links used. One year, all the food bloggers are writing about cupcakes and the home decorating bloggers are painting chairs yellow; the next year the bloggers are baking cake pops and painting chairs blue. These trends aren't isolated to the blogosphere, of course, but increasingly trends flow between mainstream media and blogs – and often the bloggers are ahead of the magazines.

Let's say there are two dozen popular fashion blogs, but they all go to similar shops, watch the same designers and only read one another's blogs. Remember Granovetter: this is an example of a closed social network, where A and B and C all know each other equally well. Such a network will have difficulty getting new information – unless there are weak ties between some of the members of the network and a different network that has access to different information. In such a network, following Granovetter, the most valuable node will be the one that brings in new information through connections with other groups of people.

Distributed conversations

The internet was designed as a *distributed* network, where each computer is connected to a number of adjacent computers rather than to a single, central hub. This structure was detailed in an often-cited memorandum, later published as a scientific paper, by Paul Baran (Baran 1964). One of the reasons for Baran's recommendation of a distributed network for the internet was that such a network was thought to be more likely to remain functional in the case of an attack on it than a centralized network would be. In a centralized network, the entire network would go down if the central hub malfunctioned.

The relationship between mass media and their readers, listeners or viewers can be compared to such a centralized network where one central hub connects to many individual nodes, but where nodes cannot connect directly to other nodes. Blogs, on the other hand, are organized as a distributed network. There is no central hub: instead blogs link to a number of other individual blogs.

The network of blogs isn't equally distributed in the way Baran's network is portrayed in Figure 3.2. Some websites receive far more links from blogs than others. Obvious examples of sites that become hubs in the network of blogs are sites like Technorati, Digg or Blogger, which are all sites that are not themselves blogs but which index blogs, provide general links to popular blogs, or are platforms that people use for blogging. Individual blogs are not equal nodes in the network either: some are far more popular than others. There are several sites that list the most popular blogs, organized either by the number of readers or by the numbers of links pointing to them. It's easier for search engines to count links than to count readers, as information about visitors to a blog is only registered by the server hosting the blog, and so is not publicly available. However, there are rating services, such as Alexa. com, that have volunteers who use their software when they surf the internet, so that Alexa can see which sites their group

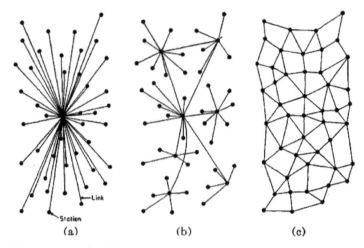

Figure 3.2 On the left (a) is a diagram of a centralized network where all nodes connect to a single central hub. This structure is also called a star structure. In the middle (b) we see a diagram of a decentralized network, while (c) shows a distributed network (Baran 1964).

of hopefully typical web users visit most frequently. Based on their statistics, Alexa calculates an approximate number of visitors that major sites likely attract. Links, on the other hand, are easier to count, but do not necessarily translate into visitors.

There is a vast difference between the popularity of the ten or hundred most popular blogs and that of the tens of thousands that follow. Most blogs only have a handful of other blogs linking to them. These are the 'long tail' of blogging (Anderson 2006). Despite each of these blogs having only a few readers, all of them put together have more than the *New York Times* has readers or the BBC has viewers. At the other end of the spectrum, BoingBoing.net, consistently one of the most linked-to blogs online for the last several years, has 50,000 inbound links.

The vast difference between the most popular blogs and most other blogs can be described by a phenomenon known as the power law (Barabási 2012; Shirky 2003). Simply put, the power law states that blogs that already have 'power' will get more. This is not a feature specific to blog or social networks; it is a feature of networks, as physicist and network theorist Albert László Barabási explains:

> A new node joining a network, such as a new web page or a new protein, can in principle connect to any pre-existing node. However, preferential attachment dictates that its choice will not be entirely random, but linearly biased by the degree of the pre-existing nodes – that is, the number of links that the nodes have with other nodes. This induces a rich-get-richer effect, allowing the more-connected nodes to gain more links at the expense of their less-connected counterparts. Hence, the large-degree nodes turn into hubs and the network becomes scale-free – the probability distribution of the degrees over the entire network follows a power law. (Barabási 2012)

Preferential attachment thus causes an already popular blog to get even more popular, in much the same way as protein P53 clusters in a 'cancer hub'. Network theory is being used by scientists like Barabási to understand everything from blogs to cancer to traffic patterns.

Writing about social media in particular, Clay Shirky argues that the power law is a common pattern in new social systems such as those we have seen develop online in the last few decades: 'A new social system starts, and seems delightfully free of the elitism and cliquishness of the existing system. Then, as the new system grows, problems of scale set in. Not everyone can participate in every conversation. Not everyone gets to be heard. Some core group seems more connected than the rest of us, and so on' (Shirky 2003). In the blogosphere, power often translates to links. If you have a lot of other bloggers linking to you, your blog will be more easily found not only by the readers of those other blogs who follow the links to your blog, but also by search engines and sites like Technorati that index links. If I search for 'fashion blog' on Google, the highest hit will be to a site that has a lot of inbound links, because Google sees links as a kind of peer endorsement. The more links, Google's algorithms figure, the better other internet users must think the site is.

Technology for distributed communities

So the connections between blogs can be understood as digitally mediated social networks. How do these networks between blogs develop? How can people talk about blog conversations, or distributed conversations? During a panel discussion at the Media in Transition conference at MIT in April 2007, Cory Ondrejka, who at the time was Chief Technology Officer for the massively multi-player online world Second Life, argued that community can't develop in blogs because people aren't present at the same time and in the same place, as they are in a virtual world like Second Life. Blogging, Ondrejka argued, is like standing on a hill yelling into a megaphone. This is much the same argument as Plato made against writing. As we discussed in chapter 2, Plato argued that writing creates a distance between author and reader that does not exist in a conversation because you can read a text when the author is absent. That distance, Plato argued, made texts unresponsive. If you ask a text a question, it will 'preserve a solemn silence' (Plato 1999). Ondrejka's argument is seen from the perspective of the writer rather than the reader. If you blog, Ondrejka implies, you're not part of a conversation. You have no immediate access to your readers as you would do in Second Life, a chat room or another synchronous communication space.

On the other hand, what you post in a blog has persistence, whereas a face-to-face conversation or a conversation in Second Life is usually not archived for future reference. We could draw up a continuum from synchronous to asynchronous communication forms, with a printed book right over on the asynchronous end of the continuum and a live chat on Facebook or in Second Life at the opposite end. Blogs are asynchronous, but discussions in comments or between blogs can move very quickly. Twitter and Facebook conversations often move even more quickly, but older posts on these sites are also less easily accessible than the archives of most blogs.

The present tense is valued in blogs, and it is the most immediately visible aspect of blogs. The most recent post on a blog is always shown first, so a newcomer to a blog will first see what was written today, not necessarily the best post, the most popular post or the post that best represents that particular blog. A few years ago, when Technorati attempted to index all blogs, it disregarded links older than six months in its ranking of blog results, and other blog search engines likewise prioritize the new.

Old posts don't simply disappear, though. Most blogs automatically archive posts as they get pushed off the front page by newer posts. Archived posts are indexed by search engines, and while readers who simply type in the URL of a blog are unlikely to come across them, new readers will often find older blog posts about a specific topic when searching for a particular topic.

The archive also allows slow conversations. In real-time or synchronous communication media such as chat rooms, face-to-face conversations or online worlds such as Second Life or World of Warcraft, participants in the conversation must be present at the same time. If you log onto World of Warcraft five minutes after everybody else in your guild has logged off, you won't only be unable to participate in the discussions they had, you'll have no indication that those discussions ever took place – unless one of your friends logs on and tells you about it, or you read about it on the guild's web forum or mailing list. Email, web discussion forums and blogs, on the other hand, are asynchronous media because participants can communicate with each other without being present at the same time. If you read my blog five minutes after I've published a new post, you'll be able to read my post and see any comments on it.

Conversations between blogs can move quickly, and often the speed of online communication is emphasized. News, popular videos, ideas and images can spread very quickly. One of the advantages of citizen media is this speed. Major events are reported as rapidly by the people who experience them as by mainstream media. In an analysis of Twitter posts related to the 22 July terrorist attacks in Norway, the Norwegian Broadcasting Company found that the first tweets about the Utøya shootings were posted to Twitter well before mainstream media confirmed it (NRK 2011). Even mainstream media uses blog posts published by people who happen to be close to an event. During and after September 11, the tsunami in South-East Asia, Hurricane Katrina, the terrorist attacks in London and Madrid, the Arab Spring and elections and political events around the globe, bloggers who were present or touched by the events blogged their experiences. For more on this, see chapter 4.

However, the persistence of blog posts – once published, they are generally archived for months or years – means conversations don't necessarily have to take place instantaneously. In fact, Jodi Dean emphasizes the slow pace of conversations in the cluster of theory blogs she is part of, where people pick up previous ideas and make connections by linking to older posts in their own or other peoples' blogs, slowly allowing a conversation and interchange of ideas to accumulate. Blogs, she writes, 'are archives, specific accountings of the passage of time that can then be explored, returned to, dug up' (Dean 2006).

To a certain extent though, Ondrejka has a point when he says blogging is like standing alone on a hill yelling into a megaphone. When you post to your blog, you can't see your readers. Unless you receive comments, it might not be immediately obvious to you whether you even *have* any readers. How on earth do individual blogs, taken together, make a community?

At the base of the network is the simple link. Bloggers read other blogs. If I see something interesting in your blog, I'll likely write a response in my own blog, with a link to your blog so my readers can go and have a look at what you wrote.

In addition to allowing human readers to see and follow it, a link is machine readable. For instance, search engines will recognize the link as a connection between our two blogs, and many, such as Google, will interpret the link as me recommending your blog. The more sites that link to a blog, the higher Google will rank it in search results. Technorati, the blog search engine, will note that I linked to your blog, and, in addition to adding one to the score of how many blogs link to yours (thus increasing your blog's ranking on their list of popular blogs), Technorati will show my post in its list of blogs linking to yours.

Links are one-way on the World Wide Web, unlike in some earlier hypertext systems. With two-way links, a link from my blog to yours would immediately be visible on both of our blogs. This doesn't happen in basic HTML. However, bloggers can insert code into their websites that allows them to track information about their readers. Whenever you visit a website, you leave information about your IP number, your screen resolution, which operating system and web browser you use, and, if you followed a link to get to the website, the URL of the website you came from. Many bloggers check their website statistics daily, tracking how many readers they have and where they come from. This also allows them to see whether readers are coming from new places. If I made a link to your blog, and ten of my readers followed it, you might notice that your website statistics show ten more readers than usual, and that they all came from my blog. That would likely make you go and read what I wrote about your blog, and perhaps you would then link back. Today, many blogs also support a feature called Trackback. If both my blog and your blog have Trackbacks, my blog will send your blog a 'ping' when I link to you. Your blog will then automatically display a link back to my blog where I wrote about your blog. Blog posts often also display counts of how many people liked or shared a post on Facebook, or tweeted about the post on Twitter.

Facebook and Twitter as microblogs

Blogs are an open network of websites that, with crosslinks, conversations and comments, can function as a social network. There are many other social network sites where social connections are even more explicit than in blogs, and these sites have many things in common with blogs.

Facebook has been the most popular of these networks for several years, with close to a billion users in 2012. Facebook can be seen as a vast, community blogging site where your photos, status updates and links are fed into a blog that is customized for each of your friends, so they see posts from their friends. Facebook continuously tweaks its algorithms to adjust which posts you see, interspersing ads and highlighting posts according to how popular they have been with your friends. You have far less control over your Facebook feed and the way your posts to Facebook are displayed than you have with an individual blog, especially one installed on your own server, but, on the other hand, you have an active audience. It is likely that most of your friends, family and colleagues are on Facebook.

Remember the imagined group of fashion bloggers we talked about earlier? If they all only linked to each other, their blogs would be a closed network. In order to gain access to new information, members of the network need to have connections outside of the group. On Facebook, such a spread of information becomes very visible through the news feed. I live in Norway, so a large proportion of my Facebook friends are Norwegian. A lot of the items I'll see on my news feed when I log on are Norwegian. I see my Norwegian friends sharing links to news about current political or cultural events in Norway, or discussing local issues. When I was writing the first edition of this book, a common way of marking identity and personal choices and preferences on Facebook was by joining – or leaving – a group with a descriptive title. Every time you joined or left a group, that action was announced to all your friends: 'Joe joined the group <u>Peace On Earth Now!</u>';

'Jane joined the group <u>Obama for President!</u>'; 'Jack joined the group <u>Enough with all this politics, let's just party.</u>' Groups like these still exist, but today shared images and links to news stories are far more prominent in our news feeds. In five more years, Facebook will have tweaked its algorithms again and different things will be prioritized. For that matter, perhaps we'll have left Facebook and moved on to a different site altogether.

In Facebook's early days, users were automatically members of regional or university "networks". Your posts were by default visible to other members of your network in addition to your friends, and many groups were limited so only members of a particular network could join them. I saw a very concrete example of how news spread differently in different networks in the days following the college shootings at Virginia Tech in April 2007. Although the story was well covered in the Norwegian mass media, it was experienced by most Norwegians as very distant. Students and lecturers at the university I work at didn't talk about it much, and I saw no mention of it on Facebook among my Norwegian friends. However, my news feed showed me how my US friends were joining groups in support of the Virginia Tech victims. They posted icons to show their grief and wrote status messages and notes clearly showing they were thinking of little but the shootings – and small wonder, for the shocking event was far closer to them than to most Norwegians. Many of my American friends knew people at Virginia Tech. When I delved more deeply into how the shootings were affecting Facebook communities, it became clear that the system of limiting access to networks that you're not a member of made much of what is happening in other networks invisible to most users. Searching for 'Virginia Tech' and similar keywords revealed a large number of groups dedicated to discussing the massacre, but very few of these were accessible to me, as I was not a member of the networks the groups had been created in. The groups in support of the victims were not accessible to users outside of the college network they had been established in. You would see that the group existed, though, if you had a friend at that college who had joined it: 'Jason has joined the group In Support of Virginia Tech'.

Several critics of social media are concerned that we will be enclosed in a 'filter bubble' (Pariser 2011) or an 'echo chamber' (Wallsten 2005) where we only ever see others who agree with us and are never confronted with any opposition or shared debates. However, those of us who have Facebook friends from different parts of our lives or from different countries will have experienced how they share different kinds of news. I can't avoid knowing whether the local soccer team won or lost with a few soccer-loving friends on Facebook. I don't need many American friends on Facebook to witness hefty discussions about US politics. As we move into autumn in the northern hemisphere, my Australian friends post excitedly about the return of spring. These constant little reminders of differences are far more extensive than receiving the occasional letter from abroad. And of course, I can easily follow the links or look at the photos my friends post and learn more about the news and the world where they are.

Sometimes the differences between parts of your social network can be unsettling. For instance, the 22 July 2011 bombing and mass shootings in Norway completely dominated the Norwegian society and social media for many days. Facebook was used to coordinate 'rose parades' all over the country where people came together to sign and show that love was more powerful than hatred. In Oslo alone, 150,000 marched, and many, many more all over the country. In those days, it felt quite strange, almost offensive, to see all the completely ordinary posts on Facebook from people outside Norway.

There are many other social networking sites. Facebook is extensively used for informal, personal communication and of course by marketers. Instagram is a mobile-only network for sharing photographs. Foursquare lets you check in to locations and see your friends' locations. LinkedIn has a more serious and business-like tone than Facebook, and instead of setting up a profile with photos, friends and hobbies, you enter your CV in careful categories: education, honours, jobs. Instead of 'friends', you have 'connections' who can write recommendations of your work. Jobs are advertised on LinkedIn, and in some industries and regions LinkedIn is extensively used in recruiting. Others use it to find clients, collaborators or to check out someone who sent you an email, or, perhaps more commonly, they use it because everyone else seems to have a profile there.

One of the reasons social networking sites are popular is that they appeal to our instinct for collecting. New-media scholar Lisbeth Klastrup reviewed LinkedIn as though it were a computer game in a post to her blog on 19 August 2006: 'Objective of game: You can go either for the single-player mode: to gather as many connections as you can, in the shortest time possible and reach the 100% network cap (state of progress helpfully depicted in the "network" stat-bar); or the multi-player mode: to gather more "people in my network" than your fellow players.' Even social networking sites without any clear purpose apart from collecting as many friends as possible have become popular, at least for a while. Orkut, a project coming out of Google, was an example of this. Orkut was one of the first social networking sites, and it rapidly became popular among bloggers after its launch in 2004, only to be largely abandoned by them a few months later when new sites turned up. Perhaps simply seeing photos of all your friends' faces gathered on one page was a feature so satisfying that people would sign up and do it for no other reason. Orkut is also an interesting example of how the demographics of a social networking site can drastically shift. Although the early adopters were mostly Americans and other English speakers, within months of its launch Brazilian users had outnumbered the Americans two to one. Because the Brazilians wrote in Portuguese, and because messages are broadcast widely on Orkut, this led to the English speakers complaining about the onslaught of non-English speakers (Alerigi 2004). It subsequently became popular in Iran, before being banned by the Iranian government – because the dating and matchmaking were at odds with Muslim culture, the government said, though others claimed it was because Orkut allowed users to send messages to large numbers of people at once and easily share information.

Once enough of your friends have joined a social network site, social pressure can make it very difficult *not* to participate. Around 85 per cent of all college students in the United States were on Facebook as early as September 2005, according to Chris Hughes, a Facebook employee, who gave an interview published on the blog *TechCrunch* on 7 September that year. Now, many complain that so much of their social life is organized or happens on Facebook that to not participate is to be socially ostracized. Perhaps, though, Facebook and similar systems provide sites for social interaction that might not take place without the internet. In Norway, surveys have shown that students have spent less time on campus during the last five to ten years, whether due to an increased need for paid employment to finance their studies or for other reasons. This means they have less interaction with other students than previously. Facebook and other online social networking tools may help students to maintain the social connections with peers that are crucial for creating a strong learning environment. Not all university and college administrations have looked at Facebook in such a positive light, however. On finding that students spend more time on Facebook than on using the official online learning environments, some campuses have blocked access to Facebook so students cannot connect to the website from the campus network (Fort 2005). Georgetown Visitation, a girls' high school near Washington DC, reportedly not only blocked access to Facebook from the school network but also tried to frighten students away from the site: 'Our school is really interested in its image – they don't want us to be given a bad name,' says Katie, a Visitation student. She says the school brought in a law enforcement officer, who told students that 'by having a Facebook profile we are jeopardizing our future husbands' political careers' (Rich 2007). One hopes the girls also consider their own future political careers. More sensible attempts to educate teenagers about the potential dangers of Facebook and blogging include discussing the risks of revealing personal information about yourself and educating students about how easy it is to stalk a person based on the information they blithely share online (Rich 2007). Despite schools' attempts to block Facebook, censorship is very difficult to sustain and can be circumvented with fairly minimal knowledge. For instance, students can use a proxy server to access blocked services rather than connecting directly through the campus network.

As we put more and more of our lives online, privacy issues become an increasing concern. Cory Doctorow's short story 'Scroogled' portrays one possible future scenario where the massive amounts of data stored about individuals by Google and other websites provide a means for an oppressive government to control its people (Doctorow 2007). Doctorow's imagined world may not be that distant. There have already been several cases where immigration officers have Googled people upon their arrival in a country, and where seemingly unimportant information is used against them (Elatrash 2007). At the beginning of 'Scroogled', Doctorow quotes Cardinal Richelieu, who wrote in seventeenth-century France: 'Give me six lines written by the most honorable of men, and I will find an excuse in them to hang him.' While most of what we enter into Facebook may seem harmless, we should consider that it could be used in other contexts. Facebook has also had a mottled history when it comes to privacy concerns, which regularly cause Facebook users to complain, but most of us continue to use the service anyway. Several alternative systems have been proposed. There are more personal social network sites such as Path or Pair, which are intended to be more private than Facebook and only connect you to a small group of *real* friends – or in the case of Pair, only to your one best friend or lover. A different approach is taken by networks like The Diaspora* Project, which is building an open, community-based alternative to Facebook. The project was initiated by four students in New York who were directly inspired by a talk by the Columbia University law professor Eben Moglen on the privacy concerns of using a service like Facebook (Moglen 2010; Dwyer 2011). With Diaspora*, you not only own your own data, you can literally host it on your own server and still cross-post to social network sites like Facebook. Cross-posting is important because so many of us have so many of our friends and family on Facebook that the notion of moving to a new site and enticing our entire network to move as well is extremely daunting.

Publicly articulated relationships

There is a performance aspect to social networking sites that is also present in blogs, though it may be a little more subtle in the latter. When we blog or use social networking sites, we not only present ourselves as individuals, we also publicly proclaim our relationships. On LinkedIn, having influential or well-known connections is as important as having an impressive CV – or at least, that is what the interface of the website implicitly tells us.

Social media scholar danah boyd, who deliberately does not capitalize her name (boyd 2001), uses the term *publicly articulated relationships* to describe the importance of this public display of your social network. She identifies four characteristics of online social spaces that make them fundamentally different from offline social spaces (boyd 2008: 126):

1   Persistence
2   Searchability
3   Replicability
4   Invisible audiences

Blogs and social networking sites are *persistent* in that the information you enter is recorded and can be accessed later. From
offline spaces, such as a café where we're chatting with friends
over cups of coffee, we're used to informal social conversations
being ephemeral. We may remember what happened and who
said what, or tell each other stories about what happened, but
the details are rarely directly accessible. What you blog or talk
about on MySpace or Facebook will stick around, unless you
work to delete it, and deleting doesn't always work. Online
spaces are *searchable*: people can find you. Your mother or
boss can find you as easily as your school friends can. These
spaces are *replicable*: photos and conversations can be copied
and modified so there's no way of telling them apart from
the original. This is a tactic often used in bullying, but also in
political speech, as when political ads or television interviews
are altered to make a political argument. Finally, online spaces
have *invisible audiences*. You don't know exactly who is viewing
your profile or reading your blog. You can't see the audience
as you can when you're speaking to friends at a party or in an
offline public space. That means that your conversation with
a friend about a party you were at last night might be read by
your mother or teacher as well as by your friends. Additionally,
because your blog or activities on a social network site are persistent (the first characteristic), some of your audience will, in
the future, access your photos, words and activities in a quite
different context than that in which you originally posted them.

Colliding networks

One danger of online social networks is their visibility – in some
cases, they work too well. When bloggers are fired for what they
write in their blogs, or teenage daughters refuse to 'friend' their
mothers on Facebook, the problem is that two social networks
that are meant to be separate collide. Jeffrey Heer and danah boyd
have pointed out that, in offline environments, we usually keep
different groups of associates apart through 'a segmentation of

place' (boyd and Heer 2006). We meet our boss at work and our friends and family at home. We don't invite our parents to wild parties. boyd conducted extensive research on an early social networking site called Friendster. She describes how, as the site became more and more popular, more of these social spheres collided, leading people to tame their profiles to make them more acceptable to a diverse group of people. But however moderate your profile was, if your friends' profiles were not, and if your friends had left less than tame messages (called testimonials on Friendster) on your profile page, your boss or potential mother-in-law would still be shocked when they saw your profile. If you stopped linking to your friends, there's no point in being on Friendster at all.

This negotiation of multiple audiences who know you in very different contexts is also familiar to many bloggers and is the cause of many unhappy stories. Blogging and participating in social software sites often feel like participating in an intimate conversation – one may be 'famous to fifteen people', to quote David Weinberger again (2002: 104), but really, fifteen people doesn't sound very intimidating or a large enough audience to really worry about. On blogs and Facebook, it's also easy to forget about all the invisible readers, the lurkers who don't leave comments or other signs that they've been there. If you don't actively interact with certain friends on Facebook (by clicking, commenting or liking), those friends are often hidden from your news feed so that it's easy to forget that they actually have access to your profile. When you imagine who will read your Facebook or blog posts, you are more likely to think of the much smaller group of active Facebook friends than the large group of invisible lurkers. In addition to the potential invisible readers, your posts will have future readers. Digital documents tend to stay around for a long time. They are, as danah boyd notes, persistent. You might delete your blog, but it will remain for days or weeks in Google's cache, and, unless you've expressly requested it be deleted, it will probably be archived in several versions at archive.org and possibly at other sites as well. Those words you wrote when you were eighteen and furious at your boyfriend, or when you were twenty-six and hated your job, might come back to haunt you later when they're read by somebody you might not even have known when you wrote the post. Perhaps your future boss, mother-in-law or children will read what you wrote.

Closer to home, perhaps, are the cases of bloggers who have been fired because of writing indiscreet blog posts about their jobs. You'll remember from chapter 1 that Dooce was the first well-known case. Dooce worked in a technology company and hated it – and wrote funny but venomous blog posts describing why she hated it so, such as this one, written on 12 February 2002: 'I hate that one of the 10 vice-presidents in this 30-person company wasn't born with an "indoor" voice, but with a shrill, monotone, speaking-over-a-passing-F16 outdoor voice. And he loves to hear himself speak, even if just to himself. He loves to use authoritative expressions such as "NO! NO! NO! IT'S LIKE THIS!"' The post, which is still online, continued in this vein for several paragraphs, describing a variety of her co-workers and generally leaving the reader to wonder why she still worked for these people. Whether Dooce at the time considered the possibility of her co-workers and boss reading these posts is an open question, but at any rate, on 26 February 2002 she wrote about having been fired because of her blog.

Despite the media attention that mishaps such as Dooce's receive, being fired for your blog is really a rather rare occurrence, and avoiding it simply requires that you either refrain from writing things about your job that you wouldn't be happy for your boss to hear or to see printed in a newspaper. Using a pseudonym provides an added level of security for those who really don't want their social spheres to collide, or you can use services that provide levels of privacy so that posts are not public to the world. Facebook allows you to create lists of friends and make posts visible to some friends and not to others. A major feature of Google+ is the idea of 'circles', where you likewise share some things with some circles of friends but not with others. Ultimately, the best rule of thumb is to be careful about writing things online that you wouldn't be happy to say in front of your boss or your mother-in-law (future or otherwise).

Emerging social networks

Although blogs and social media appear to have developed into fairly stable forms, twenty years hence it may be clear that they were only an early stage leading to something we don't yet know the nature of. Blogs and social networking sites are both very new forms. It took half a century after Gutenberg invented the printing press for the conventions of print that we today take for granted to be set: early printers did not see page numbers, titles, tables of contents and the like as immediately obvious. Likewise, early cinema was an experimental phase and it took decades before the feature film was an established genre. Today, blogs and Facebook are mainstream, but there are many other new kinds of social media that publish semi-automated blogs about aspects of our lives.

An early location-based service, Plazes.com, tracked where users are. Registered users at Plazes set their computers to automatically send Plazes a message every time their computer was registered at a new IP address. Users typed in the name of the location (home, office, Paris, New York) and the system generated a chronology of a user's movements, displaying them to the community at large or just to the user's friends, according to the privacy settings the user had selected. If you used a laptop computer both at home and at work and connected it to wireless networks at both places, this might result in nothing more than a fairly innocuous narrative: Thursday at 08:34: Jill is at home. Thursday at 09:27: Jill is at work. Thursday at 17:51: Jill is at home. But if you travelled, or connected to the net at a friend's house or at a different café than usual, your friends would know about that, too. Plazes thus generated an automated blog about a particular aspect of your life.

Since Plazes, geo-social media have become common, with Foursquare one of the most popular. Now they use the GPS features of our smartphones instead of relying on the Wi-Fi network that a laptop computer is connected to. Checking in at a location on Foursquare or Facebook or another social media has become a kind of social sharing, mapping out favourite places with friends (Hooper and Rettberg 2011). It also generates an automatic blog describing where you have been.

Google and other search engines also track your online activities. When you visit a website, your browser tells the computer your IP number and, from that, your approximate location can usually be seen – at the least, your IP number announces which ISP you are using. If you're online from a university, your IP number contains information on which university you're at and sometimes even the specific room you're sitting in. Google stores information that connects search terms to IP numbers and may use this information in its algorithms.

If you sign up for an account with Google, thus giving it more information about yourself, it will in return give you access to the information it stores about you. You can browse back through its chronological list of what you searched for at what time, and note trends in your own obsessions and interests through days, weeks and years. If you install a special toolbar in your browser, you can even opt to tell Google about every single website you ever visit, and Google will use that information to customize your search results, attempting to find you exactly the things that it knows you like to see.

There are many other sites that allow you to track anything from the fluctuations of symptoms of a disease (patientslikeme.com) to how often you have sex (www.bedposted.com: 'For your eyes only, Bedpost offers zero social networking features other than partner logins'). You can buy step-counters and bathroom scales that connect to the internet and generate a daily overview of your activity and weight to share with others or keep to yourself and you can post your results to

Facebook or your blog. These sites generate overviews for you, displaying your data based on time – allowing you perhaps to discover that you're more likely to be grumpy at 4 p.m. than in the morning as you had thought. Self-tracking has become a fascination and a lifestyle for many, as evidenced by the blog and conference series *Quantified Self.*

When a piece of software – Google, Plazes, an iPhone app or Facebook – presents such traces of your life in chronological order, those traces become an autobiography created on the fly. This is an automatically generated autobiography, though. You wrote it – after all, you were the one who did those things, and you knew they were being recorded – but you didn't shape its narration.

In some ways, this automated journalling highlights the ways that self-documentation has always been both incidental and deliberate. Before digital cameras, people often kept their never-sorted photos in shoeboxes, along with other paraphernalia of their daily lives: tickets from trips they'd taken or shows they'd been to, cuttings from newspapers and so on. Only some of these would make it into photo albums and scrapbooks or be written about in diaries. Today's technology can write a story automatically from all these scraps of information about ourselves. Whether or not we want our stories told like this is another matter.

Imagine a complete story of every technologically mediated event in your life – every photo taken of you or by you, every phone call you've made, every email you've sent, everything you've ever written on a computer, every time you checked your email from a different computer, every game you've played. You reached level 70 in World of Warcraft on 14 May 2007; your best score in online Scrabble was 361 points, on 21 January 2011; here's that conversation on the webcam with your niece on her second birthday, and the SMS your friend sent you when her boyfriend broke up with her. Your computer would organize all this for you in the same way that Facebook organizes your relationship stories and event stories. You could choose to publish parts of your story online, as a blog that you share with others. Perhaps some sections are only available to certain people, just as a generation ago you might have had some photo albums that you would only show to certain friends. This is fairly close to Facebook's Timeline feature, which displays all your Facebook activity as a timeline from your birth up until the present, and which also encourages you to enter other significant events and photos. But this way Facebook owns all your content. If they go bankrupt, it would be lost. If they are sold, someone else will own your life story, and maybe they'll use it in ways you wouldn't like. Maybe it's already being used in ways you wouldn't like. An alternative might be an open access, distributed social network system. In such a system, you'd host your own website with your own documents, posts, photos and videos, but encoded in your site you'd have information about who could access what and about who else would be interested in which things. So you could easily let your sister have access to the recording of your latest phone conversation with her, and so on. Perhaps this is what systems like Diaspora* will really offer.

Do we want to do this? Where will systems like Facebook and blogs go in the future? Will our ability to document everything lead to us actually doing so? Participating in these kinds of auto-tracking social networks means giving up a large portion of our privacy, something we seem to be more and more complacent about doing. Perhaps that is because the return is so great: a stronger sense of belonging to a community, of belonging to a group of people who not only see who we are, but who care about us as well.

CHAPTER FOUR

Citizen Journalists?

'Freedom of the press is guaranteed only to those who own one,' wrote journalist Abbott Joseph Liebling in the middle of the twentieth century (Liebling 1960). Although freedom of speech was recognized as an important human right in the twentieth century, in practice only a tiny percentage of the population in twentieth-century democracies could easily share their ideas with more than the people immediately surrounding them. Listener and reader contributions to mainstream media such as television, radio and newspapers existed but were always positioned in carefully boundaried spaces. In talk-back radio programmes, listeners could call in their questions but would often be cut off if they said anything too controversial or rude. Letters to the editor wouldn't always be published and would always remain clearly subordinate to the editorial content of the newspaper.

In twentieth-century democratic societies, people wishing to have their words and ideas published or broadcast had to contend with editorial policies that were generally based on ideology or on what advertisers would support or the public buy. In such a media landscape, many stories would never be deemed 'newsworthy' enough to be heard. In non-democratic societies, censorship and ideological suppression by the state stopped other kinds of stories from reaching an audience. In either case, those who did not, as Liebling wrote, own a press were not able to spread their ideas. Despite the existence of an underground media consisting of pirate radio stations, 'zines, photocopied newsletters and other oppositional or small-scale, non-commercial media outlets, the mainstream media's domination of the airwaves and distribution outlets made this media subculture invisible to most people.

The internet changed one of the greatest obstacles to true freedom of the press by eliminating or greatly reducing the cost of production and distribution. By the end of the century, bloggers *could*, in effect, own a press: a modern, lightweight version of one. Blogs provide a means of publishing and distributing that is cheap and simple enough for everyone with access to the internet to use directly, whether from home, school, the library or even a mobile phone.

This new freedom to publish at will has caused journalists and editors to re-evaluate the role of mainstream, professional media. If you want more information about a current event today, you can easily search across blogs, newspapers and other sources finding stories far more diverse and extensive than those traditionally printed in a newspaper or relayed on the television news. If you're interested in the US elections, you can directly access blogs written by the candidates and their staff, you can read transcripts or videos of debates between decision makers, and opinions from knowledgeable or simply opinionated bloggers. If you're interested in the situation in the Middle East, you can not only find extensive material from politicians and political parties, you can also read the diaries of people experiencing the conflicts here and now. Nobody will vet these diaries as newsworthy or not. There is no editor deciding which diary entries to publish. However, social networks and automated indexes will make some more visible than others.

As blogs became a familiar genre, the mainstream media began to discuss whether blogging was a threat to journalism and the media as we have known them through the twentieth century. Journalists began to ask a question that kept recurring: is blogging journalism? The answer is obviously usually no: most blogs are not journalism, nor do their writers aspire to be journalists. However, whether or not individual blogs can be thought of as journalism, blogs and other participatory media are changing the ways journalism works.

This chapter will examine three general ways in which blogs intersect with journalism. First, blogs can give first-hand reports from ongoing events, whether wars, natural disasters or crimes. Sometimes, bloggers are chance witnesses to an event that turns out to be of wide interest. In other cases, the blogger is a participant in the ongoing events, such as in the case of the Baghdad civilians and US soldiers who blogged during the Iraq war, the inhabitants of New Orleans who blogged during Hurricane Katrina or the Utøya survivors who told their stories in the hours, days and months following the massacre. Often a participant-blogger takes a political stand-point and the blog and other activity in social media may play a part in the event or processes that the blogger is discussing. It can, of course, be difficult to assess how important blogs are in political processes, as we see in the discussions about the role of social media in the Arab Spring and the Occupy movement (Khondker 2011; Skinner 2011).

Second, some bloggers set out to tell stories that could have been told by traditional journalists, but where mainstream media in the view of the blogger have either failed to investigate an issue critically enough, or where the story is not deemed 'fit to print' or of sufficient interest to be publicized. These bloggers may pool resources and track down details in a way that many professional journalists do not have the time for. In these cases, blogs fulfil much the same function as journalists do. In some cases, blogs provide independent-minded journalists with a printing press of their own, free of any editor, as when Christopher Allbritton travelled to Iraq as an independent journalist, completely funded by the donations of his readers.

Third, many bloggers follow mainstream media and other blogs and filter stories according to their interests, or they carefully monitor every news item about a particular person or issue. These bloggers are filter bloggers, as described in the first chapter. Filter bloggers like these who focus specifically on topics covered in the news media have also been called *gatewatchers* by Axel Bruns. Bloggers thus represent a turn from the gatekeeping that the mass media has traditionally performed to gatewatching, as we'll examine in more detail later in this chapter.

Before looking at examples of these three ways in which blogging can approach journalism, we will examine surveys showing how bloggers themselves see their blogging in relationship to journalism. We will also consider a central tenet of journalism: the expectation that journalists are reliable and tell the truth objectively, as this is a crucial way in which bloggers, with their subjective point of view, tend to differ from journalists.

Bloggers' perception of themselves

Most bloggers do not think of themselves as journalists. In fact, in a July 2006 survey of American bloggers by Pew Internet Research, 65 per cent of those interviewed stated that they did not think of their blogging as a form of journalism (Lenhart and Fox 2006). This survey was unusual for being nationally representative. Most surveys of bloggers find their sample online, for instance by choosing to look at all blogs that link to a certain blog, or at blogs by people who respond to a questionnaire published online. These methods make it difficult to be certain that the sample chosen is representative, as the bloggers are either self-selected or show only a small area of the blogosphere. The Pew researchers instead called a large sample of Americans and asked whether they blogged. The ones who said they did were asked to answer further questions, including whether they 'engage in practices generally associated with journalism: directly quoting sources, fact checking, posting corrections, receiving permission to post copyright material and linking to original source materials out of the blog' (Lenhart and Fox 2006: 11). They found that about a third of bloggers say they 'often' tried to verify facts before publishing them and that they tried to link to their sources, while a little over 20 per cent more 'sometimes' did so. The other activities were less frequent. This means that, although only 34 per cent of bloggers think of their blogging as a form of journalism, nearly 60 per cent of them in fact 'often' or 'sometimes' try to verify facts and reference their sources. It should also be noted that 37 per cent of the bloggers surveyed said that the main topic of their blog was 'my life and personal experiences' (9) – these were diary-style blogs, and so fact-checking and linking original sources would be completely irrelevant. Only 5 per cent of the bloggers in the survey focused on the typically journalistic topics of news and current events (Lenhart and Fox 2006).

When it matters whether a blogger is a journalist

You don't need a particular degree or licence to call yourself a journalist as you would to call yourself a doctor or a psychologist. Instead, you call yourself a journalist if you work as a journalist. Until very recently, that meant that you published your writing in a newspaper or that you worked in television or radio. Today, this may also mean that you are a blogger – but if it does, that means it is much harder than previously to determine whether or not an individual is a journalist. Usually, it really doesn't matter, but sometimes the distinction can be very important – legally or pragmatically.

On an everyday level, as blogging has become recognized as an important part of the media ecology, bloggers have been more likely to receive passes to press conferences and political conventions, allowing the bloggers to report first-hand on these events rather than having to rely on reports from traditional journalism.

Many bloggers do make money off their blogging and, for some, blogging is a full-time job that supports their family.

If you blog to make money, in practice you're a professional writer and editor. As we will see in chapter 5 on 'Blogging Brands', professional bloggers will probably find themselves following most of the rules of journalism simply in order to maintain the trust of their readers and their own integrity. The ethical rules and professional conduct of traditional journalists may likewise be as much about maintaining readers' respect and trust when writing for pay as they are about higher ideals of objective truth.

At a more dramatic level, whether or not a person is seen as a 'journalist' can be a very important legal distinction. This has been most clearly tested in the United States, where journalists in many states have the right to protect their sources' anonymity, even in a court of law. Such so-called 'shield' laws vary in degree from state to state, but are often seen to be an important prerequisite for freedom of speech because, without such protection, many people would not feel safe speaking to journalists about contentious issues. In 2004, bloggers' right to withhold the identity of their sources as journalists may do was tested when a group of bloggers published information about products that Apple was planning to release. Apple sued 'John Does', that is, the unknown people whom Apple assumed had leaked Apple's trade secrets to the bloggers. Apple then claimed that the bloggers who had published the information were legally required to identify their sources, and thus reveal who the 'John Does' were. The bloggers argued that their anonymous sources were protected because they were acting as journalists, but Apple argued that they were not journalists and that the confidentiality of media sources was therefore not legally privileged. The Electronic Frontier Foundation took the part of the bloggers and eventually won the court case (Electronic Frontier Foundation 2006).

On their website, The Electronic Frontier Foundation states that they are 'battling for legal and institutional recognition that if you engage in journalism, you're a journalist, with all of the attendant rights, privileges, and protections'. Unfortunately, it is not easy to define unequivocally what it means to 'engage in journalism'.

Recently proposed legal definitions show the shift that is occurring in our understanding of what a journalist is. In the United States, several drafts of the Free Flow of Information Bill, which is intended to protect free speech by permitting journalists to shield their sources, have been discussed, although none of the many versions of the bill has become law. In a 2005 draft, people to be protected in this way were defined exclusively according to the medium in which the person published, which was required to be:

> (A) an entity that disseminates information by print, broadcast, cable, satellite, mechanical, photographic, electronic, or other means and that –
> (i) publishes a newspaper, book, magazine, or other periodical in print or electronic form;
> (ii) operates a radio or television broadcast station (or network of such stations), cable system, or satellite carrier, or a channel or programming service for any such station, network, system, or carrier; or
> (iii) operates a news agency or wire service;
> (B) a parent, subsidiary, or affiliate of such an entity to the extent that such parent, subsidiary, or affiliate is engaged in news gathering or the dissemination of news and information; or
> (C) an employee, contractor, or other person who gathers, edits, photographs, records, prepares, or disseminates news or information for such an entity. (US Congress 2005)

A later draft of the bill, the Free Flow of Information Act of 2006, proposed a definition that is significantly broader, and that interestingly enough is not tied to a specific medium:

> a person who, for financial gain or livelihood, is engaged in gathering, preparing, collecting, photographing, recording, writing, editing, reporting, or publishing news or information as a salaried employee of or independent contractor for a newspaper, news journal, news agency, book publisher, press association, wire service, radio or television station, net-

work, magazine, Internet news service, or other professional medium or agency which has as one of its regular functions the processing and· researching of news or information intended for dissemination to the public. (US Congress 2006)

Later versions remain close to this wording. While it is usually unimportant whether we regard a blogger as a journalist or not, there are times when it really matters. These legal definitions show that blogging and other forms of user-created media are causing us to redefine the nature of journalism itself. It also shows how we are transitioning to defining activities and media in a way that is not platform-dependent or dependent on the material form of distribution. A book is no longer a bound sheaf of paper, but a text that might be printed or electronic. This also shakes our media institutions. With self-publishing, what will the role of a publisher be in the future? Journalism, likewise, is no longer dependent on print or broadcasting, and that not only calls the need for paper newspapers into question, it also forces us to rethink the role of the newspaper, the television companies and radio broadcasters.

Objectivity, authority and credibility

Journalism is expected to be objective and reliable, and traditionally the editor and the brand of the newspaper or broadcaster stand as guarantee of this. Journalists are also afforded certain protections, such as (in some countries) the right to preserve the anonymity of their sources. Blogs, on the other hand, are subjective and independent, come with no guarantee of truth and do not necessarily have the same rights as traditional media. Geert Lovink describes it thus: 'There is a quest for truth in blogging. But it is a truth with a question mark. Truth here has become an amateur project, not an absolute value, sanctioned by higher authorities' (Lovink 2007b: 13).

Interestingly enough, a survey of blog readers by the

advertising company Blogads showed that these readers visited blogs precisely because they saw them as more credible than mainstream media (Blogads 2004). In this survey, 61.4 per cent of respondents stated that they read blogs because there was 'more honesty', while 50.3 per cent found the 'transparent biases' of blogs an important factor in their choice to read blogs. By traditional standards, that seems counter-intuitive indeed. How could an individual writer with no credentials be more credible than a professionally trained journalist writing for a well-established publication with a staff of editors and fact-checkers, and, not least, with a reputation to protect? Melissa Wall argues that bloggers, like mainstream media, have ways of building trust and credibility, but that these techniques are not the same:

> Just as mainstream media establish a pattern of routines to create a sense of dependability, so many of these sites seem to rely on their own distance from power for their credibility. What is notable here is that credibility seems to be established in part by characteristics that are quite different from the traditional. Many of these blogs seem to turn conventional wisdom upside down – the more personal and more open about opinions a site is, the more trustworthy and credible it will be. (Wall 2005: 165)

Blogs rely on personal authenticity, whereas traditional journalism relies on institutional credibility. We trust or distrust an article in a newspaper based on our perception of the newspaper, which is partly shaped by the society around us and partly by our own personal knowledge of the newspaper. Who the reporter is sometimes matters, but primarily it is the reputation of the media outlet that is important. Most of us are more likely to trust a news story we have read in the *New York Times* than we are to trust something we heard on the local college radio station. Bloggers build trust individually. Some of the strategies are the same as for mainstream media – for instance, a blog with professional-looking design will be more likely to convince us than a gaudy blog that looks as though it was designed by an amateur. There are countless exceptions to this, however. If Salam Pax's blog had looked overly designed, we might not have trusted it as an authentic example of an ordinary Baghdad citizen's blog. We trust or distrust bloggers based on our perception of their honesty.

This kind of personal authenticity can be faked, of course, but fakes tend to be found out in the blogosphere. Although some blogs that fake authenticity have had success for a while, they have suffered hefty negative backlashes when exposed as fakes. You can read about some examples of this in the chapter on commercial blogging, which is the field where the temptation to create fake blogging personas is the strongest.

It should also be noted that authenticity doesn't necessarily require complete self-exposure. Many bloggers, even news bloggers and political bloggers, use pseudonyms. If a blogger becomes popular enough or controversial enough, readers will likely try to figure out the blogger's real identity. When the Iraqi blogger Salam Pax was read by thousands during the US invasion of Iraq, there were lively debates as to whether he was authentic. Could Salam Pax really be an Iraqi living in Baghdad, or was he a fake? Was his blog propaganda from Saddam Hussein's government, trying to make us feel sympathetic towards the Iraqi population? Or was it propaganda from the Americans? In fact, debaters couldn't decide on whose side Salam Pax stood, and perhaps this is the most important point about this kind of direct message from a civilian in a war zone. At some level, it doesn't matter whether the blog is 'real' or 'true' or 'authentic'. It doesn't matter whether the videos of crying children and anxious mothers were *really* posted to YouTube by teenagers in Beirut as Israel dropped bombs on their city. We had already heard the news of the bombings of Beirut and the attacks on Baghdad from mainstream media outlets. The *We Are the 99 Percent* Tumblr may have a similar rhetorical function. Here, a seemingly endless stream of people post photos of themselves, no names given, holding up pieces of paper telling the story of their unemployment or underemployment or poverty, despite having worked hard. The focus here is on authentic, individual stories, but of course all or some of them may actually be invented. In a way, that doesn't matter because we know that this *kind* of story is true, and the sheer semi-anonymous mass of stories underscores that. The primary function of these blogs and videos is not to be a factual report or confirmation of what is happening. They are subjective, emotional reports on events that we already know are happening. We knew Baghdad was being invaded as Salam Pax blogged. And really, all that the Lebanese teenagers, the thousands of 99 *Percent* spokespeople and Salam Pax were telling us were things we could have imagined for ourselves – but we still wanted to read or see them from people actually experiencing the events. In this sense, the truth of blogs may have more in common with the truth of novels, art and poetry than with the facts presented by journalism.

The profession of journalism and our idea of 'news' developed as recently as the nineteenth century, when news became a commodity that could be sold and resold. Classic journalism, Melissa Wall argues, is closely tied to modernity. Wall writes: 'The values that anchored modernity were reflected in journalism: a sense that reality could be observed and documented from an objective viewpoint, an emphasis on constant change and timeliness, and a belief in being able to represent reality accurately' (2005: 154). During the twentieth century, journalism further developed in order to reach the largest number of people. One strategy was that of presenting the news as objective: 'In order to reach the largest audiences, news was presented as the mere reflection of reality, a detached, neutral report that usually included a counter point of view to any controversy so as to offend the fewest people possible' (Wall 2005: 155). In reducing discussions to two binary points of view, other perspectives would often disappear.

Melissa Wall studied a group of blogs that discussed the Iraq war and argues that they present postmodern characteristics, rather than 'traditional journalism's modern approach'. The postmodern characteristics that Wall identifies are personalization, audience participation in content creation and story forms that are fragmented and interdependent with other websites.

The traditional, modernist form of journalism is today augmented by many other journalistic genres that are subjective in various ways. Journalists are increasingly presenting themselves as participants in events, rather than assuming they can stay outside. The reporting of politics, wars and crimes is, however, still generally kept in the objective mode. For bloggers, who generally do not aspire to being journalists, trying to stay objective is completely irrelevant. This may be most apparent in the first group of blogs that approach journalism: the firsthand reports. We'll look at two rather different ways in which bloggers may end up publishing first-hand reports.

First-hand reports: blogging from a war zone

During Israel's bombing of Beirut in 2006, teenagers uploaded videos to YouTube of their families running for shelter amid air-raid sirens. In 2003, at the start of the Iraq war, blogger Salam Pax wrote almost daily of his life in Baghdad. The details he noted were of the sort that might be noted by a professional feature journalist, but the experience of hearing directly from a person who was there, involved in this horrible conflict, made reading the blog a far stronger experience than reading even an excellent article by a professional. Here are extracts from a post that Salam Pax published on 21 March 2003:

> We got two phone calls from abroad ... around 6:30 my uncle went out to get bread ... the Iraqi TV was showing patriotic songs and didn't even bother to inform viewers that we are under attack ... The Iraqi Satellite Channel is not broadcasting anymore. The second youth TV channel (it shows Egyptian soaps in the morning and sports afterwards) also stopped transmitting.

You could then move on to one of the blogs written by an American soldier participating in the war, Lieutenant Smash, later known as Citizen Smash and then as Mr. Smash. His writing was far sparser than Salam Pax's. Here's an extract from his post on 23 March 2003: 'Still working about 13–14 hours every day. Haven't had a break since Christmas. . . . Reports of deaths and casualties bring mixed emotions. Sadness at the injury or loss of fellow warriors. Relief at the low numbers reported. Hope this ends quickly. But things might get sticky as we close in on the prize.' The tense prose in many ways fits the role a soldier is expected to take: there is some manly grief, perhaps, but one needs to get on with the business at hand. Salam Pax, on the other hand, has time to worry and to write.

Salam Pax's and Lieutenant Smash's blogs are diary-style blogs – they write about what happens to them on a day-to-day basis and share thoughts on their immediate situation. Their diaries have political importance because of the significant global events they have been thrust into, one as a soldier and the other as a civilian. Their diaries have many similarities to other diaries written by people in a war zone, and such diaries have often been seen as very important documents in our understanding of wars. However, before the internet made it possible to share a diary in real time with a potentially global audience, wartime diaries were generally not read until after the conflict was over. Anne Frank's diary was retrieved by her father after the war was over and she was dead, and only then was it published. Soldiers have sent letters home but, though some of these were published while conflict was still taking place, there were no large-scale and immediate publication channels during previous wars as there are today.

When Salam Pax and Lieutenant Smash began blogging from a war zone, they were among the first bloggers to do so – and they were certainly the first to be as widely read and publicized as they were. Salam Pax, especially, became extremely popular as his site was written about in blogs and mainstream media all around the world. Although it is difficult to find exact readership figures, *Wired* (8 May 2003) and other media reported that his blog, which was hosted at blogspot.com, was so overloaded by visitors that both Blogger and Google created mirror sites that readers could visit instead. A few weeks after his blog gained such fame, the *Guardian* recruited Salam Pax as a columnist, and by the end of 2003 much of his blog had been published in book form as *The Baghdad Blog*, first in English by Atlantic Books and then in multiple translations. So in many ways the blog was tamed by mass media as Salam Pax's communication with the world was channelled into the traditional forms of mass distribution that have been honed so well through the twentieth century: newspapers and mass market paperbacks with agents arranging translations and distribution around the world. As such, one could see Salam Pax's blog as having been simply a means for him to be discovered by and recruited into the mainstream media. But although his words probably reached a different demographic through the books and the newspaper columns than they had reached through his blog, the people who only encountered him in mainstream media had a different relationship with him and a different degree of access. The immediate way in which Salam Pax's diary was originally shared with readers across the world led to a community of readers who eagerly discussed his every post and who worried about his well-being, thankful every time a new post was published to show he was still alive.

In a close reading of Smash's blog, Michael Keren argues that there was a shift from his early narratives of his experience as a civilian thrust into the life of a soldier to a kind of blogging that largely replicated the official doctrine of the US government and the standardized portrayal of war in movies and other media (Keren 2006: 93–102). For instance, he went from mentioning that he wasn't interested in attending an official Memorial Day service to posting a very traditionally patriotic message on Independence Day, and his last entry on his war experience very closely mirrors the images of soldiers returning home in movies and novels.

First-hand reports: chance witnesses

Salam Pax and Lieutenant Smash chose to blog in order to tell the stories of living through a war, as a civilian or as a soldier. They were entirely aware that their blogs would be read by many people. They were emotionally beleaguered, certainly, but were blogging with full knowledge and, it seems, a wish to share their feelings.

A very different dynamics can occur when a blogger who has mostly been writing for close friends and family is suddenly thrust into the limelight because he or she has witnessed and blogged about a major current event. A striking example was seen in the aftermath of the Virginia Tech shootings on 16 April 2007. Statistically, students are among the most likely demographic to blog, so it was no surprise to find that many of the students on campus blogged about the horrors of that day. One blogger, who used the alias ntcoolfool for his LiveJournal diary, posted the following few lines at 12:10 pm, just hours after the shootings:

> THE FIRST SHOOTING TOOK PLACE AT AROUND 7AM. I WENT TO CLASS AT 9AM. THEY DIDN'T CLOSE CAMPUS UNTIL 10AM.
> Just like that. We topped Columbine.
> Please God, have none of them be my friends. Please.

These words are moving precisely because their author is a participant in the events, and because they are so immediate: we can read them seconds after the blogger typed them and pressed the 'Post' button. Ntcoolfool posted fast and often on this day, with separate posts at 10:48 am, 11:45 am, 12:29 am, 2 pm and 4:51 pm, updates to the final post coming at 5:02 pm, 5:28 pm and 5:50 pm.

A journalist is presumed to be outside of the action, and to observe impartially and objectively. Ntcoolfool is anything but an external observer. He was, admittedly, one step removed, as he was not present in the actual classrooms where the shooting occurred, but his anger, horror and fear for his friends is that of a person directly involved in the event and has none of the distance that traditional journalism aspires to.

Blogs and mainstream media are in many ways symbiotic. The sites blogs refer to the most frequently are large mainstream media, although they refer more to blogs in total if you look at the entire list of links (Sifry 2007). Likewise, mainstream media frequently turn to blogs – and on the day of the Virginia Tech shootings, the media quickly found ntcoolfool's LiveJournal and started leaving comments asking him to call them. The first comment on a post ending 'My friends could be dead. Tears continue' is from a journalist with CBC Newsworld who writes: 'Hi This is [journalist's name] from CBC Newsworld. We are looking for witnesses right now for live phone interviews. Please call me [phone number] ASAP THANKS!' The next comments are from readers complaining at the crassness of the journalist's advance, but this doesn't deter other journalists from posting similar comments on the same post. Ntcoolfool himself doesn't directly respond to this discussion in his blog, but an update to his 4:51 pm post clearly expresses the dilemma that a chance bystander to an event can experience on having their blog suddenly the centre of global media attention:

UPDATE (5:50):
This is ridiculous. I find myself getting excited because I'm on the news (Fox News recently shared the blog). Each time I hear something else I get a brief moment of selfish joy before I am stabbed in the heart, realizing that I deserve no credit and that lives are gone, destroyed, and in pain. What is the significance of all this? My postings are simply what I always do – except I left my thoughts for the public instead of just my friends. This run of emotions is hard to bear. I need to go for a walk – but of course, what good is that since everything is outside my door. There is no escaping. The chains have been tied to the door.

Interestingly enough, another site where students at Virginia Tech shared their feelings and experiences was Facebook.

As mentioned in chapter 3, the default at the time was that Facebook posts could only be viewed by a user's friends and their college or regional network. Because of this limited viewing, the discussion of the Virginia Tech shootings on Facebook was a far more local affair than ntcoolfool's blog. News crews couldn't easily gain access to blog posts and other media shared on Facebook because access was limited to other students at Virginia Tech. On LiveJournal, ntcoolfool could have chosen to make his posts about the shootings private or visible only to his friends, but he explicitly chose to make them public, wanting to share his thoughts with more people. He also appears to have handled his brief media fame quite well, based on other posts he made that day. However, the intensity of suddenly being thrust into extreme media attention can be very stressful for a blogger who is used to having a small and intimate audience, and journalists should be very aware of the ethical issues of approaching bloggers who are in crisis as ntcoolfool was on that day. As the comments from other readers of ntcoolfool's blog show, bloggers and their readers are quick to see journalists as exploitative, in contrast to regular readers who see themselves as supportive. This is in part because of the rift between the two separate spheres (a rift discussed further in chapter 5, in relation to the *lonelygirl15* videos on YouTube). Likewise, bloggers should be very aware that when they blog, what they publish may become a great deal more widespread than they had imagined. This can of course be extremely empowering but also, sometimes, very difficult to deal with.

Salam Pax, Lieutenant Smash and ntcoolfool are all examples of bloggers who were direct participants in events that were seen as extremely newsworthy by mainstream media, and that the general public was hungry to know more about. As participants, they made no attempt to be objective. The traditional journalistic creeds of credibility and fact-checking were of no relevance to them. Their strength was instead their authenticity – but it is a different kind of authenticity than the promise that 'this is true' given by mainstream media. This authenticity is evidenced by the immediacy of the bloggers.

Bloggers as independent journalists and opinionists

The second way that blogs approach journalism is when bloggers more deliberately set out to tell stories that might also be told by journalists.

Christopher Allbritton was a freelance journalist who had spent some time in Iraq before the 2003 invasion. In March 2003, he asked the readers of his blog, *back-to-iraq.com*, to fund a return trip to Iraq, promising that, in return for donations, he would give readers frequent updates on his trip and genuine news from an independent journalist on the spot. The idea of having an independent journalist in Iraq was appealing at a time when mainstream media was 'embedding' journalists in the US army, which allowed greater insights into army working but also made it harder for the public to see the reports coming from these journalists as unbiased. But the greatest attraction of Allbritton's plan to travel to Iraq as a journalist directly funded by his readers was the promise of direct communication. In the months leading up to the project, Allbritton spent a lot of time on his blog, writing carefully researched articles and responding directly to reader questions. Readers who donated to his trip were placed on an email list where they received his reports from the field several hours earlier than regular blog readers who had not contributed money, and readers were also encouraged to submit comments and to suggest topics they'd like Allbritton to cover. Allbritton succeeded in raising US$15,000, enough to fund his trip, although his visit only lasted a few weeks due to security issues. He returned to Baghdad in May 2004, but again the expenses of maintaining basic security, paying a driver and so on led him to work as a conventional freelance journalist for the mainstream media instead of continuing as an independent journalist. Despite the apparent untenability of independent reader-funded journalism in a war zone, the experiment was successful to a point, and it's possible that similar strategies will be developed further in the future. Journalists have successfully crowd-funded investigative journalistic projects on sites like Kickstarter, which didn't exist in 2003, but not primarily using blogs.

Another conventionally newsworthy subject is politics, and there are many bloggers who write extensively about politics – as noted in chapter 1, in the 2006 Pew internet survey on bloggers, 11 per cent of the bloggers interviewed stated that their main topic is politics (Lenhart and Fox 2006). Most of these bloggers link to and comment on information published in the mainstream media or directly on politicians' websites and campaign websites. They may focus on being watchdogs, tracking everything done by or written about a particular candidate or issue. Frequently, their posts will take the form of opinion pieces or contributions to a debate – either among bloggers or among the public at large.

Some of these bloggers have gone to great efforts to obtain direct access to political events. The US Democratic Convention in 2004 was a breakthrough for bloggers wanting press access, as three dozen bloggers were given press credentials to the convention (*New York Times*, 26 July 2004). Since then, bloggers with well-established and serious blogs have frequently gained press access to similar events.

Gatewatching

The third way in which journalism and blogging intersect is through a practice that Axel Bruns calls gatewatching (Bruns 2005). Gatewatching is a term that plays upon the idea of gatekeeping in traditional media. 'At its most basic,' Bruns writes, 'gatekeeping simply refers to a regime of control over what content is allowed to emerge from the production processes in print and broadcast media; the controllers (journalists, editors, owners) of these media, in other words, control the gates through which content is released to their audiences' (2005: 11). There are three different 'gates' or stages involved in this gatekeeping, and each gate contributes to keeping traditional journalism a closed process. First, there is the input phase, where news is gathered – but it is only gathered by staff journalists. Second, there is the output stage, where news is published – but there is a closed editorial hierarchy that restricts what will be published. Third, there is the response stage, where readers comment on the news – but there is an editorial selection of which letters or responses will be made public.

This closed system is collapsing in today's world of participatory media, and we are seeing alternative systems cropping up instead, such as gatewatching. Bruns defines gatewatching as 'the observation of the output gates of news publications and other sources, in order to identify important material as it becomes available' (2005: 17). This kind of observation frequently happens in open news sites or collaborative blogs where readers submit stories they have spotted in the media, and a group of editors or a system of collaborative filtering organizes the stories so that some are shown prominently on the site to be shared with everyone. Digg.com is one such site, although only some of the stories shown on the first page of Digg are conventional news stories. The sharing of links to news stories on Facebook or Twitter is another form of collaborative filtering, as the more of our friends discuss a news story, the more likely it is to show up in our feed.

Blogs written by individuals often perform this kind of gatewatching by virtue of their linking to sources:

> This practice of outwardly directed referencing is virtually identical to gatewatching, of course (if, where done by individuals, largely ad hoc and non-systematic), and we have already made a similar argument for the importance of gatewatching in collaborative news sites – there, too, the inclusion of links to primary and additional outside resources plays the role both of enabling readers to check the accuracy of reports for themselves and of highlighting that in spite of any personal

> opinion which authors of news reports on the site may have expressed they have the intellectual honesty to open up the news process to outside scrutiny. (Bruns 2005: 180–1)

However, while blogs written by individuals do frequently link to mainstream media, they also tend to link to other bloggers' commentary on those news stories, and so they are less dominated by this gatewatching function than are larger community sites such as *Slashdot* or *Kuro5hin*.

In the years after 2005, when Bruns wrote his book on gatewatching, traditional or professional media have also increasingly moved towards a gatewatching model. In a later article that Bruns co-wrote with Tim Highfield, they explain that

> professional and citizen journalists and commentators watch the gates of newsworthy organizations whose information is relevant to their specific interests; they capture and compile that information as it is released; and they process and curate such information with an aim to publish news stories and comments which build on it. Professional journalists may still be able to follow up by calling sources and spokespeople for additional statements, while such courses of action may be unavailable to unresourced non-professionals; professional gatewatching therefore results in a comparatively greater number of news stories, whereas bottom-up, independent gatewatching tends to focus more strongly on compiling and commenting on available information. Gatewatching itself, however, is a core practice for both groups. (Bruns and Highfield 2012)

As some bloggers have moved closer to the practice of traditional or, as Bruns and Highfield call it, 'industrial' journalism, mainstream media are likewise becoming more bloglike, for instance by giving greater space to opinion and commentary as the news itself is already available. Twitter has also become a site where professional journalists and others interact on more equal footing. Bruns and Highfield write that 'Previously, industrial journalists and citizen journalists may have remained at some distance from one another, with few direct personal contacts; now they well and truly occupy the same shared space, as a heterogeneous group if not a homogeneous community' and conclude thus: 'The journalism – the collaborative pro-am journalistic coverage – which emerges from this is a shared journalism, one which no longer belongs to news organizations or news audiences alone.'

Bruns's discussion of blogs as potential gatewatchers largely emphasizes the role that blogs serve in filtering the news, that is, in determining which news stories readers actually end up seeing. However, some of the most interesting examples of gatewatching in blogs occur when bloggers act as watchdogs of the media, finding errors or omissions in the reporting conducted by mainstream journalists. In these cases, a feedback loop between blogs and mainstream media is established, where the bloggers use existing news stories to break new news, which then in turn is reported on by the mainstream media.

One of the most famous of these occasions was the so-called 'Rathergate' scandal in 2004. The popular anchor of CBS Evening News, Dan Rather, presented a set of documents that were critical of President George W. Bush's time in the military. Rather announced that the documents were from the 1970s and that experts at CBS had confirmed them as authentic. Within hours, however, bloggers had begun to question the authenticity of the documents and the typography, arguing that the font used in the documents did not exist in the 1970s. The story quickly fed back into the mainstream media and ultimately led to Dan Rather being demoted.

Another blogger who dug deeper where mainstream journalists failed is Swede Magnus Ljungkvist. Shortly after the announcement of a new government, in 2006, the mainstream media discovered that Maria Borelius, a newly appointed minister, had several years previously used nannies for her children without paying the taxes she was supposed to pay as an employer. When questioned on this by journalists, Borelius answered that she hadn't been able to afford it at the time, and the journalist took her answer at face value. Ljungkvist was more inquisitive, and searched the minister's tax records – in Sweden, tax records are available for public searching online – and found that her income during the period that she had the nanny had been far above the average Swedish income. He published this in his blog and received a lot of attention from other bloggers, and eventually from the mainstream media which followed up on the figures Ljungkvist had found. Shortly thereafter, Borelius resigned as minister, and the following year Ljungkvist was awarded a national award for citizen journalism.

Both the Rathergate and the Ljungkvist/Borelius affairs show how tightly intermingled blogging and mainstream journalism can be. Blogging and journalism are often seen as in opposition to each other, and both these stories can be told to illustrate that the bloggers 'won' over traditional journalism. However, it is equally clear that in both stories there is an interaction between the traditional and the unruly.

Ljungkvist and the Rathergate bloggers were, in Axel Bruns's term, gatewatchers, although they went a step further than simply watching and republishing the news. Bloggers like these follow mainstream media closely, and when mainstream media slip up and make a mistake, they pounce on it, do their own independent research and publish their version of the story. They can do this because ordinary citizens today have an unprecedented ability to do such research – we have easy access to many databases and archives that would have been inaccessible to ordinary citizens just a decade or two ago. In addition, bloggers have access to community. If an issue generates interest in the blogosphere, many minds can think together in ways that can be extremely powerful, as the Rathergate case shows.

Symbiosis

Much of the literature on blogs is enthusiastic about the ways in which blogs empower ordinary citizens who previously have not had access to the media or to the public sphere. Blogs have allowed people to share ideas and build resistance in non-democratic countries such as China where censorship is heavy but blogs are able to slip through, and they were important in the Arab Spring. Blogs allowed us to read the thoughts of a young man in Baghdad during the invasion of Iraq and to read the immediate response of another young man whose classmates were shot at Virginia Tech – and this immediate connection with people in the middle of globally reported events appears to bring us closer together. Bloggers have seen themselves as an alternative to mainstream media, and as a force that can reform and change the ways we conceive of media: today, anybody can own a press. Anybody can be the media.

(handwritten margin note: we saw this w/ coronavirus & the Dr forward that came)

However, blogs and social media serve the purposes of mainstream media as well. The mainstream media were quick to republish blog posts written by the young man at Virginia Tech, and to interview him. The mainstream media recruited Salam Pax to write newspaper columns. Some newspapers offer free blog hosting and use the best posts as free content for the newspaper. They ask readers and viewers who have been present at newsworthy events to send in photos, videos and reports that are then integrated into the mainstream news story. Many journalists keep their own blogs. One such journalist, J. D. Lasica, writes that 'many journalists who blog are doing just that – exposing the raw material of their stories-in-progress, asking readers for expert input, posting complete text of interviews alongside the published story, and writing follow-up stories based on outsiders' tips and suggestions' (Lasica 2003). Newspapers now run their own 'blogs', giving minute-by-minute reports from court cases and other ongoing live events, or posting short opinion pieces, or providing a long-term focus on a specific issue.

Another way in which blogs can be said to support mainstream media has been expressed by Geert Lovink: 'Blogs test. They allow you to see whether your audience is still awake and receptive. In that sense we could also say that blogs are the outsourced, privatized test beds, or rather unit tests of the big media' (Lovink 2007a). This argument is perhaps most useful in so far as it inverts the common utopian argument that blogs empower readers and viewers, allowing us to create media instead of simply consuming it. Lovink asserts the opposite: that blogs are the servants of the mainstream media, simply providing a more nuanced form of audience survey at no cost to the media. Trying to think of blogs as nothing more than this allows us to also see the absurdity of thinking of blogs as nothing but citizen journalism, empowering the bloggers.

Bloggers may be amateurs, but in many cases that is a benefit, not a disadvantage, as Lawrence Lessig argues: 'Blog space gives amateurs a way to enter the debate – "amateur" not in the sense of inexperienced, but in the sense of an Olympic athlete, meaning not paid by anyone to give their reports' (Lessig 2004: 44).

Yochai Benkler, in his influential book *The Wealth of Networks*, notes that, while professional journalists working for mainstream media appear to have a great many advantages in comparison to bloggers, bloggers have their own advantages:

> [C]learly the unorganized collection of Internet users lacks some of the basic tools of the mass media: dedicated full-time reporters; contacts with politicians who need media to survive, and therefore cannot always afford to stonewall questions; or public visibility and credibility to back their assertions. However, network-based peer production also avoids the inherent conflicts between investigative reporting and the bottom line – its cost, its risk of litigation, its risk of withdrawal of advertising from alienated corporate subjects, and its risk of alienating readers. (Benkler 2006: 264–5)

Obviously, blogs are many different things. What appears to be clear, however, is that blogs need mainstream media, and that today, the mainstream media also need blogs.

CHAPTER FIVE

Blogs as Narratives

The best blogs tell stories. People have always told stories, adapting to whatever medium was available. Novels evolved with the technology of the book, and feature-length movies grew out of the early years of experimentation with cinema. The medium of a narrative offers certain constraints and affordances. Some things are required or easy and some things are impossible or difficult in any given narrative. For instance, fairy tales come out of oral storytelling, and so they are designed to be remembered and retold from person to person – or perhaps more correctly, the fairy tales that have been passed down orally are the ones that were easy to remember and to retell. One way that fairy tales help us remember them is by using fixed formulas, like 'once upon a time' and 'happily ever after'. They have a standard set of characters fulfilling fixed and familiar roles: the princess, the wicked stepmother and the fairy godmother – or as a structuralist might say, the hero, the opponent and the helper (see, for instance, Greimas 1966). Narratives in novels and feature films have different rules, as do soap operas and reality television. You may not think of a 'story' in a newspaper or on television news as narrative, but journalism too has a deep structure almost always followed. Just like a fairy tale, a story that is deemed 'newsworthy' needs to have a problem, a hero and a villain, or at least two clear opposing sides.

Blogs are an *episodic* genre and this leads to particular kinds of narrative structure. Soap operas and episodic television dramas are another familiar form of episodic narrative. One of the most well-known literary examples of episodic narrative is Dickens's novels, which were first published in weekly and monthly instalments in journals. Blogs are personal in a way that serial television and novels are not, though, and so have even more in common with another episodic genre: the traditional paper diary. In this chapter, I will discuss blogs as episodic narratives, as well as discussing the personal narration we see in blogs, and I will round off by talking about the grey areas between fictional blogs and blogs that are hoaxes.

Goal-oriented narratives

The most obvious difference between narrative in a blog and in a novel is that the stories in blogs are told in brief episodes. Each post in a blog has a beginning and an end, and can in principle be read on its own. Read together, the posts create a larger story.

Episodic narrative is an established format that we know from soap operas, television serials, comic books and serially published fiction. However, the cliffhangers that we are familiar with from these genres, the excitement of the 'to be continued' coming in the middle of action, does not generally occur with blogs. A blogger often does not plan out the large story arc of the blog in advance, but writes from day to day, especially if the topic of the blog is the blogger's own life and experiences.

Some blogs do have a very clear dramatic arc, as when a blogger starts a blog with a clear project in mind. One amusing example of such a blog was *The Date Project*, a blog set up by a young man who was determined to find a girlfriend. On 4 June 2002, in his second post, he set himself three rules:

> One: I will strike up a conversation with three different people I do not know each day.
> Two: I will attend activities, events, or other situations where I can meet new people at least twice a week.
> Three: I will ask out at least one woman each week.

The blogger, who simply called himself 'Anonymous', blogged his progress as a way of keeping himself accountable. However, on day two of his project, a friend set him up on a blind date with 'K', and by day twenty-seven, Anonymous shut down *The Date Project* with the following words: 'It's over. I am in love, "K" and I are happy, and life goes on.'

While this is of course a highly successful project for the anonymous blogger, as journalist John Hiler notes, it is not a particularly satisfying narrative for his readers:

> I'm realizing that the whole fun of dating blogs comes from vicariously experiencing the frustrations and humiliations of the dating circuit. It's no fun when someone finds true love in, say . . . twenty-seven days (?!). It's like Bridget Jones getting married in the first chapter, or Carrie Bradshaw meeting Mr. Big in the first season (oh wait, that one did happen). (Hiler 2002)

Happiness, of course, is 'the death knell for any dating blog', as Hiler wryly remarks.

The narrative structure of a blog like *The Date Project* is always projected forwards. There is a goal that is clearly expressed when the blog is started, and that is often even summarized for new readers in the sidebar or the tagline. The blog will end when – or if – the goal is achieved. Dating blogs aren't the only kind of blog that set up this kind of project. A presumably fictional blog called *She's a Flight Risk* used the premise of a very wealthy heiress who had run away from home to avoid a marriage she didn't want. The blog is no longer at its original URL, but if you look it up in archive.org, the wonderful site that archives large chunks of the internet, you'll find that the sidebar of the blog announced the premise in brief: 'On March 2, 2003 at 4:12 pm, I disappeared. My name is isabella v., but it's not. I'm twentysomething and I am an international fugitive.' Here a clear starting point is defined with a clear goal: to escape her father. At the same time, this is a narrative premise that suits blogs because of its emphasis on process – running away – rather than on a short-term goal.

Dieting blogs are another kind of blog that use this format. A clear goal is set, and the public diary is used to keep the dieter accountable. Yet there is flexibility in this form of diary as well, as Diane Greco noted in her blog, *Narcissism, vanity, exhibitionism, ambition, vanity, vanity, vanity*, on 25 February 2004:

> By and large, the blogs tell success stories. They have to – blogging as a literary form supports the idea of eventual success. When there's bad news from the bathroom scale, the open-endedness of blogging makes it possible to cast the gain as just a temporary setback, not a failure. Diet blogging recasts or reimagines the yo-yo effects of a diet as a surface, a space, a site for potentially endless re-inscription. Dieting as Etch-a-Sketch, very postmodern.

As blogging has become professionalized over the last few years, an increasing number of blogs actually do plan the larger story arcs across several posts. In an attempt to make regular posting easier, bloggers may set up fixed weekly posts. *Miss Minimalist* posts reader stories every Monday. Every Friday, SouleMama and many other crafts bloggers post a single photo and a short text that is repeated, word for word, every Friday:

> {this moment} – A Friday ritual. A single photo – no words – capturing a moment from the week. A simple, special, extraordinary moment. A moment I want to pause, savor and remember.
> If you're inspired to do the same, leave a link to your 'moment' in the comments for all to find and see.

In a way, this pause from the usual daily narration of text and images lends a lyrical quality to the blogs that participate. The crosslinks between the different bloggers who follow the {this moment} Friday ritual lends a sense of shared pause and reflection to these blogs.

Ongoing and episodic narration

In his dissection of narrative desire, Peter Brooks writes of the '*anticipation of retrospection* as our chief tool in making sense of narrative' (Brooks 1984: 23). We read with a certainty that there will *be* an end, and that when we have reached it, we will be able to look back and see the whole. We read because we desire the end of the story.

When blogs tell stories, they generally do so in an episodic form, with each post being a self-contained unit that contributes to an overall narrative. Each post makes sense in itself, but read together – not necessarily in sequence – the posts tell a larger story. That story is usually partial and incomplete and does not form a narrative whole as well-formed stories in mainstream literature and cinema do. Instead, the overall story as gleaned from reading a blog is likely to be pieced together from fragments, perhaps supplemented by bits of stories from other places.

Episodic narratives are particularly well suited to our style of reading on the internet. Usability guru Jakob Nielsen has notoriously pointed out that users *don't* read on the Web; they scan and skim (Nielsen 1997). Although it has become a commonplace to claim that 'I hate reading on a screen', we're certainly spending more and more time with texts on screens. Emails, online newspapers, weblogs, online shopping, Facebook and other familiar screen texts don't usually follow Nielsen's 1997 rules for bullet lists and bold keywords, but they do provide reasonably brief nuggets of text that each make some sense on their own. Until lightweight tablets and dedicated reading devices became common a few years ago, most of us were not happy reading 500-page blockbusters on our computer screens, but, well before the Kindle was released, we were already spending hours reading and moving between fragments. Today, we see blogs positioned between the long format of ebook readers and the speed of pressing a 'like' button on a ten-word Facebook comment or posting a photo to Instagram.

Weblogs are an obvious example of the success of serial narrative on the Web. Most posts in weblogs are short enough to be read in a few minutes. Instead of watching a 22-minute episode of a television serial each week, a weblog is read in two- or ten-minute sessions once a day or once every few days or at irregular intervals. Added up, regular readers of a weblog spend a considerable number of hours perusing their favourite blog over the years.

In chapter 1, we looked at Jason Kottke's blog, *kottke.org*. His blog, along with *MegNut*, the blog of his wife, Meg Hourihan, shows how such an overall story can be pieced together by a regular reader. The development of Kottke's and Hourihan's relationship, as seen through their blogs, is neatly chronicled by Rebecca Mead in a story she wrote for the *New Yorker*. Mead relates how readers heard briefly of Kottke and Hourihan living together in San Francisco before moving to New York together. A year later, readers of *MegNut* and *kottke.org* who read between the lines might have pieced together a less rosy picture:

> [W]hen Meg took off for Nantucket in the summer of 2004, the move was conspicuously undertaken in the first-person singular. In December 2004, she wrote a post entitled 'A Sad Breakup'; and while its subject was Barbie, whose boyfriend, Ken, had sometime earlier been sidelined by Mattel for a new beau, Blaine, attentive readers wondered whether a more significant allusion was being made. . . . Meanwhile, Jason was blogging moodily about hiring a man with a van to move his stuff across town. (Mead 2006)

Things looked better the following year. Although neither Kottke nor Hourihan explicitly mentioned their relationship, they both mentioned a trip to Ireland at about the same time. In November 2005, Hourihan announced their engagement on her blog, and the following March she posted their wedding photo. Some time later, they became parents. There was little mention of the pregnancy on their blogs, but a few days after the baby was born, both Kottke and Hourihan posted photographs of their son on their blogs, along with brief announcements. The baby and his little sister, who was born a couple of years later, only show up in their blogs very occasionally. For instance, Hourihan, who since changing professions from technology to cooking mainly blogs about food, published a post about food choices during pregnancy a little after the birth announcement for their son, while Kottke, as we saw in chapter 1, jokingly compared the baby's reflexes to the accelerometers of new electronic gadgets.

Bloggers often avoid writing directly about their emotional and personal affairs. Neither Hourihan nor Kottke write confessional or diary-style blogs. Their blogs are filter blogs with a preference for certain topics. Kottke writes about technology and design, while Hourihan's blogs have shifted focus over the years, from web technology to food to frugal living. Back in 2004, the two bloggers didn't blog that they had broken up – but observant readers might piece together the pieces if they followed the blogs over a long period of time.

Other bloggers share more of the juicy details of their lives, and frequently link back to key posts. When bloggers write over many years, new readers can click back and forwards through their archives, piecing together the story – or at least, *a* story – of their lives. Some bloggers, like Penelope Trunk, are especially good at linking back to the key points of a story in the blog archive. Penelope Trunk writes career advice at her blog, and her often controversial advice is offered in a very idiosyncratic, personal manner. Her style of writing is almost abrasively honest, and she has a seductive way of twisting a story that starts off with a personal confession into general advice for the workplace, combining anecdotes from her life with links to research that back up her argument. Let me give you an example from a fairly typical post. 'I am trying to figure out what is the right kind of guy for me to be dating now that I'm getting a divorce,' she started a blog post on 13 May 2008. She continues to wryly describe a bad date, while poking some fun at herself at the same time. She decided not to date this guy any more, she writes, because he wanted an alcoholic wife, like his first wife whom he constantly complained about: 'It is [. . .] obvious to me that he will marry another alcoholic. He likes that in a girl.' She mentions her own marriage to a man perhaps too similar to herself, and links back to key blog posts about what went wrong and about her divorce. Then, after linking to articles on other sites about research studies that have found that we mirror the people we spend time with, the post deftly turns to career advice: 'So if you are complaining that you are in an office with people who are terrible at what they do, ask yourself why. And instead of broadcasting that you chose to be with terrible people, do some self-reflection and figure out why, so you don't do it again.'

Trunk's website states that she writes career advice syndicated in 200 newspapers, and certainly her writing style would often work as writing for traditional media. But her blog becomes far more than the sum of its individual posts because of her skill at interlinking her posts. She constantly links back into her archives, weaving her posts together and encouraging the reader to read more, to get more engaged in her story, and thus to want to return to hear more. Sometimes the feeling is that of witnessing a train crash, as when she posted a photo of her bruised, naked thigh on a hotel bed, on 28 December 2011: 'I am at a hotel. I think I'm dying. I have a bruise from where the Farmer slammed me into our bed post.' She talks about surviving domestic violence as a child. The post engendered over 600 comments, many telling Trunk to leave her boyfriend immediately. The next post, on 1 January 2012, explains why she's not leaving 'the Farmer', and, as so often, she connects her very personal life choices to her career advice: 'People like what I say because I show them how they can fix anything when they take responsibility for fixing it. That's what I truly believe. And that's why I'm staying with the Farmer.'

Penelope Trunk uses her personal stories to shock us into reading. Her style is very different to the far less confessional styles of Jason Kottke and Meg Hourihan. And yet, her blog isn't exactly a diary. It genuinely does primarily offer career advice, which also often uses shock as a rhetorical strategy, and she doesn't only link back to personal posts in her archive; she also very frequently links back to career posts. Her posts use a lot of links, both to her own archives and to external sources.

There are certainly many career bloggers who are less con-fessional than Penelope Trunk, but popular blogs written by individuals tend to share some sense of the blogger's story. Amanda Soule writes *SouleMama*, with daily posts about her life as a mother of five on a farm they have recently bought. Her very popular blog has weekly sponsors and is an impor-tant channel for creating and maintaining interest in Soule's books about crafts, creativity and family. Another blog in the same genre is Meg McElwee's *Sew Liberated*. McElwee writes about sewing for kids and about bringing up her two young children in a Montessori-inspired home, and like Soule, she writes and sells crafts books and online sewing courses. Other craft bloggers sell crafts kits, knitting patterns, online work-shops or crafted products online.

Blogs like these tend to use a lot of photographs in their posts. The photos fill the whole width of the main column, and there are often a whole series of them, with commentary that is often more about expressing an emotion, an impression or a fragment of a life than about conveying information about events. In this way, these blogs are often more lyrical than nar-rative. In a typical post on *Soulemama*, a series of photos of items on a breakfast table (a cup full of steaming tea, a bowl of porridge, flowers in a vase) is followed by a brief text: 'As the kettle whistles, oatmeal cooks and eggs bake, slowly they make their way into the kitchen on this sleepy, dark, rainy morning – one by one, youngest to oldest, as happens to be the order today. And in this way, and at this table, our day together begins' (12 August 2012). There are also posts about how to do a particular craft activity with kids, or how to sew some-thing specific, or about a new book project or a friend's new book.

Blogs written by groups of people, such as *Boing Boing* or *Mashable*, tend to be less personally revealing, and there is little narrative structure to these blogs. They are far more closely related to the news media or to a more or less carefully curated cabinet of curiosities than to personal narrative.

Justin Hall's blog *Justin's Links* is a far more deliberate narration of the blogger's life than are the blogs we have considered
so far in this chapter. Hall is a pioneer of online journalling,
and began writing his life online in 1994 (Hall 2004). As Rob
Wittig relates in a review of *Justin's Links*, the temporality of
the site was always a major narrative hook:

> I'll never forget the Monday morning in the mid-90s when I
> rushed in to work (my only internet connection at the time,
> imagine!) and hurriedly pointed my browser to www.links.
> net to see if Justin Hall had broken up with his girlfriend
> over the weekend. I didn't know Justin personally. Still don't.
> But I had been enjoying his groundbreaking Web diary for
> several months, had turned some co-workers on to it, and all
> of us had gotten swept up in Justin's inner (and quite public)
> turmoil as The Big Conversation loomed. (Wittig 2003)

Wittig continues by noting how when he returns to reading
Justin's Links, years later, the freshest posts have elisions that
whet his curiosity, pushing him to read more in order to fill in
the holes in the narrative as best as he can. Justin writes:

> Riding the 11.10 pm bus from Tokyo into the country-side
> the navel of Japan Gifu that's both hotter in the summer and
> colder in the winter, where we will gladly step off at 5am in
> the country where we might have her mom take care of us
> some, meaning we'll have only family things to worry about,
> as the rest of life will be limited to 33k slow bauds through
> expensive everywhere slow wireless japan. (*links.net*, 14
> November 2002)

Wittig asks, hungry for more: 'Who is the new "her" of "her
mom?" How long has he been in Japan? I must read on!' One
of the main fascinations of this kind of narration is that the
narrative moves in the same time frame as that within which
our own lives play out.

This is a different brand of narrative desire to that which
Peter Brooks maintained was triggered by novels. While
Brooks discussed the novel reader's desire to reach the end,
a blog reader's desire is instead always for the next post. The

blog reader hopes that there is no end. An end would not tie up all the loose ends, answer the questions and make the narrative into a neat, comprehensible whole. It would simply be a barrier between the reader and the story. The reader would know that the story continued, but without the reader being able to access it. As Phillippe Lejeune writes of diaries, 'All journal writing assumes the intention to write at least one more time, an entry that will call for yet another one, and so on without end. . . . To "finish" a diary means to cut it off from the future' (Lejeune 2001: 100–1).

Most blogs end when their writers simply stop writing. Sometimes this is explained. Some blogs were set up for a specific project, such as losing weight (*Tales of a Bathroom Scale*), having a baby in the face of infertility (*A Little Pregnant*), finding a girlfriend (*The Date Project*) or paying off debts (*We're in Debt*). When the goal is achieved, the blog often ends. Sometimes the blogger feels that they have developed a persona in the blog that traps them, not allowing them to write as they now want to write. Dr. Crazy's blog, *Chronicles of Dr. Crazy*, was an example of this. For a semester, the blogger who called herself Dr. Crazy wrote primarily about life as a young, single academic who wants to have a sex life and still retain academic respect. After some time, she posted a final post to her blog, writing:

> For a long time now, I've felt somewhat hemmed in by the space that I designed in the blogosphere. The pseudonym that was supposed to give me freedom in fact limited me: because of the voice that I had chosen for 'Dr. Crazy,' and because of some of the things that I had chosen to write, I felt like I had to be very careful about what I revealed about my work. I had aimed, in the beginning, to compose a blog that allowed me to look at the personal and the professional in conjunction, but that was not what I'd achieved. What I'd achieved was the construction of a space, identity, and voice, that allowed for me to talk about personal life things but that ultimately stripped me of all authority (and of all ability to defend my positions) about the professional. (*Chronicles of Dr. Crazy*, 4 January 2006)

This blogger chose to quit publishing *Chronicles of Dr. Crazy* and instead start a new blog where she could establish a new voice allowing her to write differently.

Sometimes a specific event leads a blogger to quit. Justin Hall, one of the most prolific personal bloggers ever, put a stop to his personal blog, *links.net*, by posting a tearfully emotional ten-minute video in January 2005 describing his distress about the blog, struggling with his inability to combine his deep need to make media, write, publish and share, with his need to have meaningful relationships and love. In the video, he describes how important blogging is to him and talks about the dilemma this poses when people he cares about don't want him to write about them: 'Because I can't write about people because they don't want to be there and I have nothing to write about . . . and I publish my life on the fucking Internet and it doesn't make people want to be with me, it makes people not trust me and I don't know what the fuck to do about it' (Hall 2005). Hall didn't delete his blog archives, but hid them for a while so that you needed to know the URL or to have found him via a link or a search engine to find the blog posts. Hall resumed blogging a few years later, though far less frequently and revealingly than he once did.

The most final ending of all is death. When a blogger dies, the blog does not necessarily come to an immediate end. Often, the software allows readers to continue to post comments. Sometimes a relative or friend will post a notice on the blog to tell readers what has happened. Regine Stokke was a Norwegian teenager who blogged about her battle with cancer. She died in 2009 and in the following months her family posted photos of her grave, first one taken immediately after her funeral and later a photo of the grave covered with flowers on the day that she would have turned nineteen. Regine's family also published a book compiled from her blog posts, which sold very well. Many blogs, like Regine's, become memorials to the blogger, filled with messages from friends, family and readers, much as we are becoming accustomed to seeing social media profiles become memorials when their owners' die (Brubaker and Hayes 2011). Other blogs simply disappear, deleted when the bill to renew the domain goes unpaid.

Blogs as self-exploration

Viviane Serfaty characterizes weblogs as simultaneously mirrors and veils (Serfaty 2004). Just as we study ourselves in a mirror, shaping our features so our reflections please us, so we create a reflection of ourselves in a weblog. At the same time, we use our blogs to veil ourselves, not telling all but presenting only certain carefully selected aspects of ourselves to our readers.

Pseudonymous blogs often play a flirtatious game of peek-a-boo, showing but not showing all. For instance, the pseudonymous blogger may tell us about funny episodes (this guy I saw at the coffee shop!) or life-altering concerns (the birth of a child, a long-distance move, a divorce, a new job, a lost job) in a tone of voice as though she were writing to a close friend. Regular readers come to know the characters and places in the blogger's life, and easily forget that there are also myriad experiences and thoughts that the blogger deliberately doesn't share on his or her blog. Often pseudonymous bloggers post photographs to their weblog, cropped to only show themselves from the chin down, or with their eyes blocked out, as if wearing an inverted veil. Pseudonymous blogs often have no links to archives. They exist in the moment, an autobiography of now yet, to regular readers, there is a long history and a feeling of slowly growing to know the author. That, of course, is largely due to our susceptibility to stories. As Wolfgang Iser pointed out in the seventies, readers are experts at filling in the gaps (*lehrstelle*) in a narrative (Iser 1988).

A pseudonymous blog like *Chronicles of Dr. Crazy* was a clearly personal blog about its author's life and thoughts, and posts regularly appeared that were explicitly for the purpose of thinking through a topic important to the writer. Sometimes she asked for advice or opinions, and commenters were often supportive and helpful. Blogs that stick to discussing topics outside of personal, day-to-day experience can have a similarly self-reflective function, as Rebecca Blood, a pioneer blogger, wrote in an early essay on blogs:

> Shortly after I began producing *Rebecca's Pocket* I noticed two side effects I had not expected. First, I discovered my own interests. I thought I knew what I was interested in, but after linking stories for a few months I could see that I was much more interested in science, archaeology, and issues of injustice than I had realized. More importantly, I began to value more highly my own point of view. In composing my link text every day I carefully considered my own opinions and ideas, and I began to feel that my perspective was unique and important. (Blood 2000)

We might think that a personal blog such as *Chronicles of Dr. Crazy* or *Justin's Links* gave a more comprehensive picture of the blogger than Rebecca Blood's or Jason Kottke's filter-style blogs, but the bloggers' own experience is clearly more complicated than this. Blood describes her blog as being a useful self-reflective tool, allowing her to see sides of herself that she hadn't fully realized the importance of. In this respect, her blog was like the mirror Serfaty refers to. Dr. Crazy, on the other hand, finds the image of herself portrayed in her blog obscures a crucial part of her personality, namely her professional authority. Her blog became a veil that hid part of what she wanted to explore. When pseudonymous bloggers post photos of themselves that show some of their faces, but not all, or that show themselves only from behind, they simultaneously use their blogs as mirrors and as veils – exploring themselves, hiding parts of themselves, and looking through the veil to communicate with their readers.

Fictions or hoaxes? Kaycee Nicole and lonelygirl15

We generally assume that blogs are reasonably accurate representations of the blogger's life, but of course, blogs can be entirely fictional. One of the first widely publicized cases of a fake blog or diary was that of Kaycee Nicole, who presented herself as a high-school student who was fighting leukaemia. Kaycee became more and more popular, and developed and maintained friendships not only through her blog, *Living Colours* (no longer online), but also through email and in chat rooms. In time, Kaycee's mother Debbie started a companion blog about caring for a child with cancer. When Kaycee eventually died in 2001, her online friends were devastated. However, not long after her reported death, some bloggers started seeing inconsistencies in her story and began wondering whether she might have been a hoax. Much of the discussion and detective work that led to Kaycee's exposure as a fake is documented in a *Metafilter* discussion thread started on 18 May 2001 (acridrabbit et.al. 2001). When Kaycee's friends found out that both Kaycee and Debbie were fictional, they were furious. They felt deceived and used (Geitgey 2001; Powazek 2001; Woning 2001).

The Kaycee Nicole case was neither the first nor the last time fictional characters have been presented and interpreted as being real. Orson Welles's radio production of H. G. Wells's *War of the Worlds* in 1938 is the most well-known example of widespread belief that a fiction is true. Welles's Halloween joke was taken as fact by thousands of listeners, who panicked, believing that Martians had attacked planet Earth and annihilated much of the United States. Welles had dramatized the science fiction story as though it were being reported live on radio. The radio play started with introductory music, leading listeners who had turned on their sets after the introduction that explained it was a play to assume that this was a standard news radio broadcast. The music was interrupted by announcements that abnormal activities had been observed on Mars, and then that Martian troops had landed in New Jersey. The radio play became more and more dramatic, with the radio reporter instructing listeners to seek open spaces and avoid congested areas, and it culminated in a description of gigantic Martians striding across the Hudson River and demolishing New York. By this point, reports hold that many listeners had already fled their homes and did not hear the following announcement that the show was fiction. According to one survey, as many as 28 per cent of listeners believed that the play had been a real news report (Cantril, Gaudet and Herzog 1966).

Both *War of the Worlds* and Kaycee Nicole mimicked media genres that were fairly new at the time, that of the radio broadcast and that of the confessional blog. Neither genre is used predominantly for fiction; in fact, most radio broadcasts are explicitly factual and most blogs are sincere reports of an actual individual's ideas or experiences. Most of the fiction we encounter is clearly delimited – a novel is enclosed between the two covers of a book and is clearly labelled as a novel. Movies are watched with a set of rituals around them clearly telling us what is part of the fictional movie and what is not. We usually watch movies in a cinema or on the full screen of a television or computer. Additionally, movies also use title sequences and end credits much as novels use covers, title pages and tables of contents: to show us what is part of the fiction and what is not. In new genres such as radio in the 1930s and blogs at the turn of the twenty-first century, such conventions were not established. In the case of blogs, they may never be established, as the Web does not present closed, whole works in the same way as books, movies and even television with its clear schedules tend to do. The Web is not part of the Gutenberg parenthesis that we discussed in chapter 2. On the Web, we read in fragments – maybe we spend five minutes a day checking a favourite blog, wander around looking at YouTube videos for twenty minutes, read some emails and then follow a link to a website that a friend recommended. This means that fiction is not always clearly marked as such. Or even if it is, we might not see those signposts because we haven't read the entire diary or seen all the videos on the YouTube channel.

While Orson Welles and Mercury Theatre on the Air created *War of the Worlds* as fiction and as art and entertainment, the anonymous woman who created Kaycee had no obvious motive. She did not make any money out of the elaborate fiction. On the contrary: she sent generous presents to many of her – or rather Kaycee's – online friends. Kaycee's creator put a lot of time and care into building and maintaining relationships with her readers. She poured emotions into the role she acted, crying on the phone to van der Woning, for instance, when she was playing the role of Kaycee's mother Debbie (Woning 2001). For the actual woman who performed as Kaycee, Kaycee was fictional. She constructed and found a set of objects that she used as props in her own game of make-believe: photos of the girl next door, various websites, presents. Kaycee's name, personality, age and the nature of her illness were basic tenets that determined what was possible within this fictional world.

A later fictional blog that also received a lot of publicity was the video blog *lonelygirl15*. Lonelygirl15 was the user name of a 16-year-old girl, Bree, who posted video blog entries to YouTube every few days during the summer of 2006. At first, her videos seemed unremarkable, much like the many other video diaries kept by teenage girls on YouTube, but, as time went on, her story became stranger and stranger. She was home-schooled, and her parents were very restrictive. More ominously, her family were members of some kind of a sect or cult, and Bree had been chosen to take a prominent part in some ritual they were planning. This involved a lot of preparation on Bree's part, including strange dietary requirements and learning an ancient language. Bree had a good friend, Daniel, who also posted videos to YouTube, and both Bree and Daniel actively took part in the YouTube community, participating in discussions in their comment sections and mentioning other popular YouTubers. Bree also had her own MySpace profile, and exchanged emails with fans and friends from YouTube. By the end of the summer, *lonelygirl15* was one of the most subscribed-to channels on YouTube.

But in September 2006, after much speculation among her fans, lonelygirl15 was revealed to be a hoax, a carefully scripted narrative created by screenwriters and film-makers Ramesh Flinders and Miles Beckett. Bree was not, in fact, a 16-year-old girl, but was played by the actress Jessica Rose. Daniel was likewise played by an actor, and Bree's emails and comments were written by Amanda Solomon Goodfried, a supervising producer and supporting actor (Hefferman 2006).

In contrast to the case of Kaycee Nicole, *lonelygirl15* was designed as a fiction from the start, and the characters in the videos were hired actors. However, the videos were not explicitly announced as fictional, and it was not until viewers revealed that the story was not true that the creators came forward and admitted that they had created *lonelygirl15* as an experiment in new forms of cinematic storytelling. After being exposed, they continued to produce the series for a while, though now explicitly as a fiction. They experimented with various ways of making money from this kind of online fiction, such as product placements, and there have been spin-offs, such as an alternative reality game based on the series and a sister series, *KateModern*.

When Kaycee Nicole and lonelygirl15 were revealed to be hoaxes, readers and viewers were furious. The main reason, of course, was that people felt tricked. They had been treating Kaycee Nicole and Bree as peers, as people like themselves. They had invested emotionally in Kaycee Nicole's illness, and in Bree's difficulties, and many had written heartfelt emails to the characters, had chatted online with Kaycee or recorded video messages for Bree, giving of themselves and offering support and care. This participation goes beyond what we feel for characters that we know to be fictional. Yes, we cry over novels and movies, and we sit on the edge of our seats begging horror movie heroines to 'look behind you!' or 'turn on the light!', but we're protected, emotionally, by the knowledge that it's just make-believe. That protection wasn't there for the readers and viewers – and participants – who truly believed that Kaycee Nicole and Bree were real.

A related sense of anger was expressed by popular video blogger Paul Robinett, who uses the YouTube handle Renetto. Robinett followed *lonelygirl15* eagerly and was horrified to find out that it was a fake. He posted a very emotional video in response to the news. Here's a transcript of some of what he said:

> Look, YouTube is only for people like me, that film in good lighting and in bad lighting, and in my house but in my yard, and you know, I say uh all the time. Uh, and uh. And I don't edit my videos and I don't put really cool music to my videos, like lonelygirl did. No wonder, cos she had a whole freaking production team! No wonder she's like the second most subscribed! And no wonder she gets millions and millions of video views, it's cos she's cheating! And it makes me sick! . . . YouTube's not for fake stuff! It's for real stuff! . . . Kick her off of YouTube, she doesn't belong here. (Robinett 2006)

To Renetto, *lonelygirl15* is cheating, and that's not fair. The point isn't that she's fake, it's that she's gaming the system – 'no wonder she's like the second most subscribed!' Lonelygirl15's fans and Kaycee Nicole's friends thought that they were on an equal footing with these fictional characters. When they found out that they weren't, they felt that they had been used.

Whether they are fictional or not, narratives in blogs differ in several ways from traditional print or cinematic narratives. They are episodic and are published in the same time frame as that of their readers. They are generally not driven towards an ending, towards closure, as traditional narratives are. And as we have seen in the cases of Kaycee Nicole and lonelygirl15, the boundaries between fiction and hoax are far more shaky – and contentious – than in most traditional narratives. As blogs become more and more common, they may develop more conventions that make them less susceptible to these anxieties about truth and fiction. We may also see more blog narratives that are explicitly fictional (Thomas 2006) and that never attempt to fool their readers.

CHAPTER SIX

Blogging Brands

If you search a bookstore for books on blogging, you'll quickly find that most of them are about how to make money from blogging: *Blog Marketing: The Revolutionary New Method to Increase Sales, Growth, and Profits*, by Jeremy Wright; *ProBlogger: Secrets for Blogging Your Way to a Six-Figure Income* by Darren Rowse and Chris Garrett; and *Blogging For Income: The Fast Track Plan For High Traffic and Big Profits* by Brandon Connell are just a few of the titles published in recent years. To be fair, we should also mention titles like Tara Frey's *Blogging for Bliss* or even Lambert Klein's self-published but highly ranked *Blogging for Pleasure and Money*, which also focus on the joy of blogging.

Businesses use blogs in their marketing as a way of improving customer relations and establishing a popular presence on the Web or as a way of getting attention. Individual bloggers make money from advertisements on their blogs, often starting blogs about specific topics that they hope will generate lucrative ads and affiliate sales. Spammers create fake blogs, often using software to automatically generate them, creating link farms where the fake blogs link to the websites the spammers are trying to hype and that search engines then assume are popular because of all the links.

This chapter explores these uses of blogs, in particular focusing on how blogs work in marketing. We'll look at specific examples of how individuals make their blogs into businesses and how businesses use blogs to connect with customers. We'll also consider questions of integrity, trust and authenticity and how or whether these can coexist with 'monetizing' blogging. This discussion will be informed both by statements from bloggers themselves as they consider adding advertisements or accepting sponsorship deals, and by Mark Andrejevic's more theoretical discussions of exploitation of our work and engagement in blogs and other social media. First, though, let's consider the way social media have changed our expectations as consumers.

The human voice

'Markets are conversations.' That phrase is taken from *The Cluetrain Manifesto*, a manifesto of ninety-five theses published online in 1999 by Rick Levine, Chris Locke, Doc Searls and David Weinberger. *Cluetrain*, which was expanded and republished as a book the following year, was aimed at businesses operating in the 'newly connected marketplace' of the internet but was also broadly read and referenced by bloggers and academics. It argued that the internet was changing the market and the ways in which consumers communicate about products, and that these changes were occurring a great deal faster than any taking place in the companies trying to sell to that market. Looking back, *The Cluetrain Manifesto* seems both impressively prescient and quite self-evident and is an excellent reminder of how much has changed in the last decade or two.

The idea of the internet as a conversation has been strong ever since, and it is echoed in Robert Scoble and Shel Israel's popular book about corporate blogging, *Naked Conversations* (2006). Thinking about selling something into a conversation, whether it be news stories, movies, iPods, cars or fashion, is a very different thing from trying to sell something to an audience. As people spend more time online, they spend less time on other media. This means that the tried and tested sales strategies of previous generations – television advertising, for instance – aren't working as well as they used to.

'Markets are conversations', the first thesis of *The Cluetrain Manifesto* reads, and the list continues: '2. Markets consist of human beings, not demographic sectors. 3. Conversations among human beings sound human. They are conducted in a human voice.' *The Cluetrain Manifesto* is a challenge to corporations to communicate honestly with consumers:

> 14. Corporations do not speak in the same voice as these new networked conversations. To their intended online audiences, companies sound hollow, flat, literally inhuman.
>
> 15. In just a few more years, the current homogenized 'voice' of business – the sound of mission statements and brochures – will seem as contrived and artificial as the language of the 18th century French court.

The Cluetrain Manifesto didn't mention blogs because blogs, at the time, barely existed. In 1999, advertising online was largely limited to banner ads on popular websites. 1999 was also the year that blogging began to become popular, and, by then, web discussion boards, chat rooms and email had brought the conversational web to mainstream audiences as well as to the pioneers of Usenet and BBSes. Consumers had begun to turn to each other to discuss products they were considering buying, or had bought, or liked or hated. Amazon.com had been in business for four years and customers were getting accustomed to comparing other customers' reviews of products before making a purchase. The dot com bubble had not yet burst, and expectations were high.

'The market' was becoming interconnected, with television viewers discussing plot turns with hundreds or thousands of other viewers online, readers writing reviews of books they'd bought at Amazon.com and people discussing good or bad customer service in online discussion groups and mailing lists. *The Cluetrain Manifesto* demanded that big business and big media answer back, in the same human voice that the audiences and consumers were using.

The Cluetrain Manifesto was written from the point of view of consumers who were thrilled with the growing communication with their peers but frustrated at corporations' lack of understanding of these new conversations. *Cluetrain* argues that corporations need to take part in online conversations because these conversations already exist – and if corporations don't get involved, they'll become irrelevant. Today, businesses know this, and most attempt to have an active presence in social media. Mistakes and omissions are certainly still made, however.

Social media have forced corporations to rethink PR and marketing. Trevor Cook, a publicist, argues that blogs finally free corporations to speak directly to consumers, rather than having to always go through journalists (Cook 2006). While blogs in many ways liberate corporations from the media, the direct communication with customers and clients in a blog or other social media also means that publicists have to develop different strategies to those that had become standard over many years of working with mainstream media. Because publicists have traditionally had to find a way to get the media to publish their stories, they have learnt to focus sharply to attract journalists' attention. Journalists are trained to look for conflicts and inconsistencies, and to find problems. Sensibly enough, journalists don't want to be mouthpieces for corporations; they want journalism to be critical, and so they try to find gaps in the publicists' stories. As Cook points out, the necessary response of publicists is to obsessively eliminate anything negative from the way they represent the products and companies they're trying to sell (Cook 2006: 48). That leads to the hollow, untrustworthy voice of PR that *Cluetrain* argues so strongly against.

Cook argues that, as publicists begin to engage directly with blogs and bloggers instead of only being able to reach the public through the mainstream media, they will have to 'accept some of the roles and responsibilities traditionally associated with good journalism. That means emphasizing qualities like fairness, balance, accuracy, and integrity in our own materials rather than slanted, hyperbolic advocacy that ultimately relies on the third-party endorsement of a trusted media brand for its credibility' (Cook 2006: 52).

Interestingly enough, this connects to our discussion of blogging and journalism in chapter 4. Ultimately, it seems the question of whether blogging is journalism has to do with money. If you blog to make money, that means your profession is writing and editing: you're a professional writer and editor. In order to maintain the trust of your readers and your own integrity, you will probably find yourself following most of the rules of journalism. And as we saw in chapter 4, most bloggers do follow basic journalistic rules such as attempting to verify facts and citing their sources (Lenhart and Fox 2006). Looking at the commercial sides of blogging, it is clear that professional bloggers also need to maintain trust, for instance by clearly separating sponsored content from the editorial content, and by maintaining a sense of what Cook calls 'fairness, balance, accuracy, and integrity'.

In the following, we'll explore ways in which individual bloggers make their blogs into small businesses, earning money from advertising, sponsorship, micropatronage and paid referrals. We'll then see how large corporations and small businesses have used blogs both in marketing campaigns and in long-term strategies for branding and customer relations. Finally, we'll look at some of the cases where commercial blogging has gone wrong and done more harm than good – which brings us back to *The Cluetrain Manifesto*'s authentic human voice, and to Cook's call for 'fairness, balance, accuracy, and integrity'.

Advertisements and sponsored posts on blogs

Many of the most popular blogs are commercial in the sense that they make some amount of money from ads on their blogs. There are no clear figures for how much bloggers make, although there is a great deal of variation. There are certainly many people who are able to make a living from independent blogging, and there are many more who aspire to do so but fail to, or who are happy to augment their incomes by a little ad money or to receive free samples from companies trying to spread word about their products. According to a 2007 survey conducted by University of Texas researchers in collaboration with Chitika, a company offering advertising systems for bloggers, bloggers made half a billion US dollars in 2006 (Mookerjee and Dawande 2007). That figure is fairly low, considering the global reach of blogs, and the figures are likely to be inaccurate, given that the overall estimates are solely based on earnings for blogs that used the Chitika system. The researchers simply took an educated guess at the blogs' other earnings. But when you consider that the first commercial blogs only appeared a few years before this survey, the earnings estimate from the Chitika survey is noteworthy – and responses from bloggers suggest that they were not far wrong. One interesting point emphasized by the researchers was that blogs in their survey didn't appear to follow the expected 80/20 rule, where 80 per cent of the money is expected to be earned by 20 per cent of the products or companies. Instead, the top 15 per cent of blogs, based on Technorati's ranking at the time, made 90 per cent of the money. Perhaps that's partly because the long tail of bloggers – the amateurs who simply enjoy blogging – don't bother with ads because they see their blog as a hobby rather than as a profession.

An increasing number of bloggers *are* seeing their blogging as a profession, however. Bloggers who are able to make a living from individually run blogs usually either have a strong personal brand built up over years, or they seek niche markets to blog about, where advertisements and affiliate programs that match the products they discuss will pay well, or they use their blog to support and build a market for other products or services such as books or classes.

Heather Armstrong's *Dooce.com* was one of the first blogs that made enough money from advertisements for the blogger to live on a 'comfortable enough middle class to upper-middle class income' as Armstrong told *The Salt Lake Tribune* (Canham 2006). The history of her site gives us an interesting history of early commercial blogging. The first ads that Armstrong included were text ads, that is, small text-only advertisements, managed by a company called AdBrite that allowed advertisers to buy ads for a particular length of time on a particular website. Another system is contextual ads, where the advertiser and blogger aren't matched per se, but where the ad itself is matched to the content of the webpage displaying the ad. Thus, a blog post about attending a wedding might bring up ads for wedding products and services, whereas a blog post reviewing a digital camera would likely bring up ads related to photography. Ads can additionally be customized to the individual reader's geographic location, which is revealed by the reader's IP number. Even greater customization is possible if the reader is logged into Facebook or Google while visiting a blog, which allows ads to be targeted according to pages liked on Facebook or searches done on Google. Google's AdSense, launched in 2003, was the first major program offering bloggers and other website owners easy advertising. Google bought Blogger in 2003, and in 2005, AdSense was integrated into Blogger.com's user interface, making it very easy for Blogger users to add advertising to their blogs. Today, most blogging platforms either make it easy for bloggers to add advertising, or the blogging platform automatically displays ads and the revenue goes to the blog host, not the individual blogger. Some services, like blogg.no, have a system where the most popular blogs get a cut of the site's overall advertising revenue.

Armstrong found that she didn't make enough money from text ads alone, and so in 2005 she added graphical advertisements to her blog as well, which quickly increased her income. She wrote about her reasons for this in a post on 21 September of that year, explaining that she and her husband needed the money and were planning to live on the income from the blog exclusively in a transitional period. After this rather apologetic section, she gives a more positive rationale as well:

I also think that right now is a perfect time for me to go for it, to publish myself and make a living while doing it. There are examples out there of 'publishing empires' where one person owns several Internet properties and hires people to maintain those properties for him: car sites, gossip sites, gadget sites, your garden variety boobie sites, etc. You know who they are. What's so exciting about technology and the state of the Internet RIGHT NOW is that I can hire myself and maintain my own property. And so can anyone else, it's just a matter of working to make it happen and taking control of the power.

Armstrong got a lot of complaints from readers about her decision to add advertisements to the site. Many of the complaints, which she discussed in a post on 1 November 2005, were about the sheer size of the graphical ads, and about their 'ugliness'. Although none of the complaints she cited specifically addressed the idea that the actual writing might change as a result of the blogger accepting advertisements, Armstrong did clearly feel the need to address this concern, and she fiercely wrote, 'I'd take down my Web site before I'd let an advertiser have any say in my content.' In an earlier post on 19 August 2004, when introducing text ads, Armstrong wrote wittily though poignantly about 'selling her soul'. It is quite clear that early bloggers going commercial had a lot of conflict in their minds about changing a labour of love into a living. But despite the reader complaints, the Alexa.com graph of *Dooce. com*'s readership over time showed that the readership grew significantly in the year or two following the introduction of ads, although 2007 saw somewhat lower figures. The site continued to be popular. Armstrong was on Forbes list of the thirty most influential women in media in 2009, and was declared 'the queen of mommy blogs' by the *New York Times* in 2011. The introduction of ads doesn't seem to have discouraged readers.

Dooce uses personal stories, photographs and humour to attract her readership and is able to live off the ads on her site. Like many other bloggers, she also has other income sources. Her book about post-partum depression (*It Sucked and Then I Cried: How I Had a Baby, a Breakdown, and a Much Needed Margarita*, Armstrong 2009) was a best-seller, and she has also published a collection of the monthly letters to her daughter that she originally posted to her blog (*Dear Daughter*, 2012). Like many bloggers, she also gives talks. The books are heavily based on her blog posts, and the popularity of her blog certainly also helped launch her book projects.

While many of the best blogs are very personal, another approach to commercial blogging is to be extremely thorough, objective and serious, such as Darren Rowse's *Digital Photography Blog*, which ran from 2004 until 2009. Rowse and his team would simply scour the Web for any new reviews of digital cameras they could find, and post them all, along with a photo of the camera, a brief excerpt from the review and, of course, a link to a site where you can buy the camera in question, thus earning Rowse a referral fee. Each post followed a completely rigid format, always beginning with '[Magazine or site] has a review of the [camera model], and writes', followed by an extract from the review. The website was clearly optimized for search engines and intended to attract readers searching for information while planning to buy a new camera. There were lots of ads, and there was practically no sense of any personality. Rowse ran and still runs a number of other blogs as well, including the very popular Problogger.com, which we'll return to later in this chapter. He also runs a new photography blog, *Digital Photography School*, which has a far greater sense of personality than his first one.

Other commercial bloggers opt for humour, such as the pseudonymously written *Manolo's Shoe Blog*, where the blogger uses the character Manolo to great effect. While the blogger has never claimed to be Manolo Blahnik, the famous Spanish fashion designer particularly known for his women's shoes, he (or she?) prominently displays a quote from Blahnik on the blog: 'Manolo Blahnik Says "Manolo the Shoeblogger? Sorry, not me. But it's very funny, isn't it? Hilarious!"' Cleverly enough, this denial from the real Manolo actually adds credibility to the blog – the real Manolo likes the blog! This post from 6 August 2007 is still typical of Manolo the shoe-blogger's style. A picture of a pair of shoes is shown with a brief text beneath the image: 'Manolo says, the fall is coming, and it is time to prepare with shoes such as this simple, suede, <u>sling-back peep-toe pump the Kate Spade</u>. Not only is it elegant, but the Manolo thinks it is very smart in these two rich colors, the ruby and the navy.' The link from 'sling-back peep-toe pump the Kate Spade' goes to the item page for these shoes at Zappos.com, an online shoe store that offers so-called associates a 15 per cent cut of the total amount paid by customers who they refer. These particular shoes cost US$278, so each time one of Manolo's readers bought a pair of these shoes after clicking through from his blog, Manolo earned US$41.70. If a reader found that particular pair too expensive, but continued surfing on Zappos.com and bought another pair instead, Manolo received a 15 per cent cut of whatever the reader paid. This affiliate income is still used by *Manolo's Shoe Blog* and is common practice on many blogs today.

In addition to his income from referrals, Manolo has income from ordinary ads on his site. He has contextual ads from Google, with images, and small ads from a number of sites down through his right-hand column. Importantly, Manolo does more than simply provide links to shoes his readers might buy. He also clearly spends a lot of time reading other blogs about fashion, and generously links to other bloggers, and often to bloggers who are not particularly well known or commercialized. This active social networking is important in building a community of active readers, who not only read Manolo's blog but also leave comments, blog about Manolo on their own blogs and, of course, buy shoes.

Micropatronage

Around the same time as Dooce introduced advertisements, Jason Kottke chose another strategy for making a living from blogging. On 22 February 2005, he made an announcement on his blog *kottke.org*: 'I recently quit my Web design gig and – as of today – will be working on *kottke.org* as my full-time job. And I need your help.' Kottke explained that he was asking regular readers to become 'micropatrons' of the site by contributing a small donation. He did not set up formal subscriptions or limit access to the site for non-contributing readers, but simply left it up to readers to decide what they'd like to do. The reason for doing this was that he'd found blogging to be increasingly time-consuming and that it put a drain on other important parts of his life, and so he had considered quitting. But blogging also gave him a great deal of pleasure: 'this little hobby of mine has been the most rewarding, pleasurable, maddening, challenging thing in my life.' The problem, he'd decided, was not that he wanted to quit blogging, but that he didn't want to have to deal with two jobs: blogging and the web design job he was paid to do. He also saw it as an experiment to find ways of professionalizing blogging without accepting advertisements, and as an experiment in a new kind of patronage suited to our time: hence micropatronage where each reader pays a small amount rather than having a single, very wealthy sponsor or patron, as was common for artists in the Renaissance. This is a similar approach to that taken by Christopher Allbritton, the independent journalist who used reader donations to fund a trip to Iraq in 2003 (see chapter 4).

Kottke did manage to make enough money in donations to support himself for a year – at a little less than a third of the income that he had received from his web design job (*kottke. org*, 10 April 2005). As he admitted on his blog when the year was up, 'about 1450 micropatrons contributed $39,900' (22 February 2006). However, less than one in three hundred of his monthly readers contributed as micropatrons, and he anticipated that any future fund drives would be less successful, as many contributors had in a sense been offering back payment for the seven years Kottke had already been blogging. That led him to actually recommend advertising to others as a more sustainable model, which in some ways matches Dooce's argument, posted to her blog on 1 November 2005, for using advertising rather than a subscription model or something akin to micropatronage: 'By using ads I'm making my livelihood my problem and no one else's.'

Flattr is one of several recent systems to support micropayments for blogs and other online activities. On their website, they explain their model like this: 'Pick how much you'd like to spend per month. Then, whenever you see a Flattr button on a website that you like, click it. We count up all of your clicks at the end of each month and distribute your monthly spend between everything you've clicked on. Simple, right?' Bloggers can easily install Flattr on a Blogger blog and on other blogging systems, and so allow readers to easily donate small amounts of money when they like a post. It remains to be seen whether payment systems like Flattr or other kinds of crowd-funding or micropatronage will take off for funding blogging.

When Kottke decided not to attempt to live off his blog for a second year, he gave the following reason: 'The day that *kottke. org* becomes a real business that focuses on profit first (instead of the pseudo-business labor-of-love it is now) is the day the site will probably start to suck' (10 April 2005). Despite the moderate successes of Christopher Allbritton (the journalist-blogger we discussed in chapter 4) and Jason Kottke in funding their blogging projects through many small reader donations, few bloggers after them have attempted to copy their example. Instead, bloggers wanting to monetize their blogs, as the jargon has it, generally turn to advertising, sponsored posts and affiliate links.

Sponsored posts and pay-to-post

Micropatronage and ads surround the blog but can, in theory, leave the posts and the blogger's integrity intact. When actual blog posts are sponsored, questions of trust and integrity arise. The first high-profile example of sponsored posts arose in December 2004, when a group of fifteen high-profile bloggers were recruited by Marqui, a company that made a content management system, to write weekly posts linking to the company's site. The company did not require the posts to be positive about their product. In return, they would pay the bloggers US$800 per month. Most of the bloggers quit after their three-month contracts were up, some with no comment, but several writing that the sponsorship deal had made the whole process of blogging difficult for them. In late 2004 and early 2005, the sponsored Marqui posts caused a lot of debate. On 5 December 2004, Steve Boyd wrote on his blog *Get Real* that the paid bloggers were 'squandering the trust that people have for them'. Molly E. Holzschlag, one of the Marqui bloggers, decided not to renew her contract with Marqui because it changed the way she felt about blogging: 'Primarily, I learned that I can't blog naturally if I feel forced to do it, and that's intriguing because I can write in just about any style. But, it turns out my blog is really personal, I take it personally, and I need it to be that way' (Molly. com, 28 February 2005). Holzschlag's site is – according to the first page you see when you type http://molly.com into your browser – a site that shares her 'web development work and personal thoughts'. It is not primarily a diary-style site, and yet she found that her blog was 'really personal'. As we'll see in the next section of this chapter, the sense that your blog is less your own if you are paid can be seen as an example of exploitation (intentional or not) where the blogger becomes alienated from his or her own labour.

The divide between editorial content and sponsored ads is strict in conventional journalism. When bloggers blur that line by accepting payment to write about a product or company, they break with the cultural expectations set by journalism. There have been many examples of mainstream media getting into trouble for blurring the line between editorial content and sponsored content. One of the most famous is the payola scandal in the USA in the 1950s, when it became apparent that radio stations were being paid by the record companies to play particular music, thus making that music more popular. Today, payola is illegal in the United States, unless there is full disclosure by the radio station that the music in question is sponsored.

Blogging is an unregulated area, and this is the sort of question that shows that blogging is not simply a form of journalism. It is not entirely clear whether blogging should follow the rules of mainstream media about separating editorial content from sponsored content, and, even if there were an agreement about this, it would be difficult to make bloggers follow it. J. D. Lasica argues openly that a blogger who wishes to be thought of as a journalist cannot post sponsored entries: 'If bloggers are paid by a corporation to write about the company, they're no longer acting as amateur journalists. Journalists cannot and do not accept payments from sources' (Lasica 2005). But as we saw in chapter 4, only about 34 per cent of bloggers think of themselves as journalists (Lenhart and Fox 2006).

The Marqui blog-sponsoring was a limited experiment for bloggers who had been individually recruited. By 2006, however, there were several systems that aimed to act as brokers between bloggers willing to write for money and advertisers wishing to find bloggers to promote their products. PayPerPost was one of the most controversial but also one of the more successful. Today, PayPerPost is one of several sites belonging to IZEA, a company that sells sponsored blog posts and tweets to marketers and allows bloggers to sign up to write paid posts. At their website, IZEA promotes paid posts on minor celebrities from reality shows and the like, charging anywhere from a few hundred to several thousand dollars for a package of tweets and blog posts from, for example, several of the mothers on the US television show *Dance Moms*. IZEA describes their business as 'social media sponsorship', or 'SMS', describing it thus:

> SMS is a rapidly emerging word of mouth strategy where brands provide material compensation, such as cash, coupons, products, points and trips, to social media influencers in exchange for content through blog posts, status updates, checkins, or other unique experiences.
>
> By maintaining the authenticity of the publisher's unique voice and opinion, and adhering to the required disclosure (see: FTC guidelines), social media sponsorships fill a growing void between public relations, marketing and advertising that can be an effective and measurable part of the overall marketing mix.

As a blogger, you sign up for PayPerPost, and then have access to a list of tens or hundreds of 'opportunities' that are available. Sometimes these are very specific about how they want blog posts to appear, like this listing from October 2006:

> The post should describe about culture and how marriage affects culture. It should cover the topics., 1) Is Marriage Really needed? 2) Asians gives more value to marriage, For example in India, I see that Online matrimonial Portals are making a great income. For example, i came across, Bharatmatrimony. com, It seems to be the leader of online Matrimonial services. 3) They try several innovative ideas, like, launching of the First matrimonial toolbar, Also Provides RSS feeds., Even yahoo has shown an interest on them and has invested in them. (Opportunity 765)

A Technorati blog search at the time suggested that this attempt at generating buzz wasn't all that successful: not many blogs linked to the site. However, a year later, more than two hundred blogs did so. Most of these had low authority on Technorati – that is, not many other blogs linked to them – and many of the blogs seemed like spam, offering little but lists of links, it being unclear whether these new links were caused by PayPerPost or other strategies. Other 'opportunities' offered at PayPerPost that month asked you to plug a javascript into your blog post so the sponsor could pay the blogger extra money for each click-through to the sponsor's site. There was a Christmas gift service, for instance, which specified that in your post, with the javascript that showed top-selling gifts, you needed to include a sentence about 'how bloggers will be making money this Christmas, and not just on PayPerPost!' (Opportunity 735).

In their early months, PayPerPost received a lot of criticism for their service, in particular because they didn't, at that point, require bloggers to disclose that they were being sponsored. In fact, some of the 'opportunities' bloggers were offered specifically required that the blogger not mention that he or she accepted payment for posts. After heavy criticism, PayPerPost revised their policies and now require that bloggers disclose that they accept money for posts, although bloggers may choose whether to do that on a post-by-post basis or with a single badge for the whole site, stating that they accept sponsored posts. The rationale given for this policy was precisely the need to maintain readers' trust, as stated in the 'Code of Ethics' posted to the PayPerPost website in October 2006:

> Your readers trust you. PayPerPost is committed to keeping it that way. That's why we insist on a strict policy of full-disclosure when you discuss an advertiser's product or service on your blog. By receiving payment for blogging about a certain topic, even if you would have written about that topic anyway, you run the risk of giving the impression of a conflict of interest. By showing your audience, in a very visible and proactive manner, that you are being paid for that content, you will maintain the trust of your readers and avoid any appearance of impropriety.

In 2009, the Federal Trade Commission in the United States revised their guidelines for truth in advertising to explicitly include blogs. They require that relationships between advertisers and bloggers be disclosed, for instance by a blogger including wording like 'I received a free sample of this from a company' in their post recommending a product. Different countries have different laws and guidelines about this that may be less explicit, but often existing laws about truth in advertising will in fact also cover blogs and social media.

Sponsors also often contact bloggers directly, for instance inviting them to events specially crafted to encourage bloggers to write about them, or to ask the bloggers to write reviews of their products. Some of the events are quite extravagant, involving long-distance flights and fancy hotel rooms and of course well-organized activities designed to be fun to blog about.

Critics argue that sponsorship can change the style of a blog completely, as non-sponsored garden blogger Trey Pitsenberger writes in *The Blogging Nurseryman* on 11 May 2011:

> What do you get when you have garden blogs that are sponsored by major corporations involved in gardening? Fluff! 'Look how easily so and so handles that (insert brand here) power saw.' How about, 'excited about my newly planted (insert brand here) container garden in my front yard.' One more is, 'can't wait to cook up the delicious meals I read about in (insert brand here) book'. There is nothing wrong with writing about how well so and so looks wielding a chain saw, but do we really need to put the brand name in there? Of course, that's who you're being sponsored by.

This is probably not really what the authors of *The Cluetrain Manifesto* intended when they recommended the use of a human voice.

Many bloggers have likewise been critical of networks like PayPerPost, and yet this and similar services have continued to be successful. Blogger Lynn Terry offers one of the more nuanced positive perspectives on PayPerPost in a post to her blog *ClickNewz!* on 6 October 2006:

> Individual blogs . . . rise and fall on their own accord. If the writer consistently produces bad content, the blog will fail due to lack of readership. If the writer consistently produces great content, the blog will be a success because of that.

> Whether or not they choose to disclose revenue sources has no real impact on whether the content is good, or whether its bad. The bloggers that will rise to the top and gain substantial readership are those that have great writing style and always give an honest opinion – even if it is just an opinion, and whether its objective or not.

This ignores the non-human readers of blogs. Search engines trawl blogs and other websites for metadata that can help sort websites according to how good they are, so that the best sites can be shown at the top of the list of results you get when you search online. One important measure search engines use is the number of other sites that link to a site. If a hundred blogs link to your site, it's probably more interesting or important than a site that only has three blogs linking to it. Spammers create fake blogs or fake comments that link to the sites they're trying to push. Search engines and spam filters are, however, getting better at finding machine-generated blogs and comments, and, if caught, spammers are likely to have all their sites banned from the search engine, rendering them practically invisible online. So marketers prefer human-written content to surround the links to their sites – that way, search engines will count the links as genuine endorsements rather than as spam. Whether or not a blog has readers, and whether or not those possible readers lose faith in the blogger, search engines will continue to read the links as endorsements, and so the poorly written, dishonest blog posts bought for US$3 on PayPerPost will still be valuable to marketers who simply want to game the search engines.

Exploitation and alienation?

In the sections above, we have seen several examples of bloggers being reluctant to introduce ads or accept sponsorship of their blogs. These discussions were perhaps more common in the first decades of blogging than they are today, when we are increasingly used to commercial blogs and social media. In her book *Blog Theory* (2010), Jodi Dean uses the term 'communicative capitalism' to describe the sometimes uneasy symbiosis between our love of communicating in social media and the firm hold that commercial companies today have on our social media platforms, whether Facebook or individual blogs, saturated with ads and sponsors. Dean writes that 'communicative capitalism is that economic-ideological form wherein reflexivity captures creativity and resistance so as to enrich the few as it placates and diverts the many' (4). Our participation in social media, whether it is blogging or Facebook or Pinterest or something else, Dean argues, causes us to be exploited and controlled: 'the very practices of media we enjoy, the practices that connect us to others and ostensibly end our alienation, appropriate and reassemble our longings into new forms of exploitation and control' (29–30)

The idea of blogs and social media as exploitative is also discussed by Mark Andrejevic, who uses Marx to argue that the labour we put into our blogs and other social media can be and often is exploited and coerced by our employers, by marketers or by the social media platforms themselves. Andrejevic's main example is a service that promises to allow companies to leverage their employee's social networks (on Facebook or elsewhere online) to contact and woo prospective clients and customers, or to recruit new employees. Services like this show how our social networks are becoming assets that are literally bought by our employers when they hire us. What does it mean, though, to have our personal, social connections bought and sold? What are the consequences of our employers expecting us to share company news on our personal profiles or blogs, as is often the case today?

Andrejevic uses Marx's concept of alienation, where a worker is *estranged* from his or her labour. In Andrejevic's article 'Social Network Exploitation' (2011: 94) he quotes Marx: 'Estrangement occurs when our own activity appears as something turned back against us as "an alien power" over and against oneself.' Andrejevic cites conservative blogger

Andrew Sullivan who, as many others, lauds the fact that bloggers appear to 'seize the means of production. It's hard to underestimate what a huge deal this is' (Sullivan, quoted in Andrejevic 2010: 92). However, if we use a blog host such as Blogspot or Tumblr instead of hosting a blog on our own server, we don't entirely control the means of production. We have even less control in more closed social media systems such as Facebook or Twitter, where users have very little control over how their data are presented, distributed or reused. As Andrejevic argues, 'productive resources are in the hand of consumers, but [. . .] the means of communication and distribution are *not*.' Andrejevic is concerned that we lose control of our own work, that is, over our own blogs, blog posts, status updates, photos and friend networks. We may end up alienated or estranged from our work.

In the sections above, I've quoted several bloggers who strongly want to keep their integrity. Molly E. Holzschlag felt that she couldn't blog 'naturally' while accepting money from Marquis. In 2012, her blog is still ad-free. Other bloggers, like Heather Armstrong, find ways of making money that they can accept. A more detailed description of how a blogger can move from an initial dislike of ads on blogs to finding kinds of blogging that she feels good about can be found in Annabel Candy's post 'Blog Advertising and Sponsoring: My Personal Story' (18 October 2011) on her blog *Successful Blogging*. As many other bloggers have written, she chose not to put ads on her travel blog, *Get in the Hot Spot*. At first, her reason was that 'blog adverts look ugly' and she doubted they would make her much money, anyway. Later, she tried Google Adsense but strongly disliked it, and the reason for her dislike matches Andrejevic's description of alienation perfectly: 'Not only did I earn just AU$9.59 a month but I hated handing over control of my blog to someone else. Although Pammy Anderson seems nice enough, I don't want to see her face and cleavage on adverts on my blog. My ideal reader doesn't either.' She also describes receiving perks and freebies through blogging, such as a luxury trip to Shanghai that Coca-Cola paid for. But fun as that may be, it won't pay her bills, and this woman wants to make a living off her blogging: 'It's a social media barter system where bloggers write posts in exchange for a product or an experience. That can be fantastic but bloggers can't live on free drinks, free clothes and free parties can they? I wouldn't mind trying it but my kids might get a bit hungry.'

Finally, after running various other side businesses off her blog (selling a book, selling services and using affiliate links), she decided to sell her own ads and retain control over her blog. She describes creating a ten-page media kit describing her travel blog and its 20,000 readers a month, detailing exactly the kinds of ads and sponsored posts that she thought would be good for her blog, deliberately keeping prices high to avoid devaluing her brand. This approach was successful: 'to my surprise within one week I sold my first sponsored blog post. For US$799.' Perhaps this is a woman who has taken back control of her 'means of production' and of her own labour. She can sell her blog for more money and retain more control than by simply signing up for Google Adsense as the less successful bloggers might try to do. Andrejevic sees labour in social media as more personal than many other kinds of work, and certainly bloggers use their voices, their personal stories and their ideas more clearly than most other professions. Bloggers like Heather Armstrong and Annabel Candy are their own bosses and fight to retain control of their blogs.

Corporate blogs

Businesses that establish blogs come from the other side of the system. Businesses that blog generally don't want to 'monetize' a blog through ads or sponsorship – instead, they want to use their blog (or sponsor existing bloggers) to boost an existing income stream by generating new attention for their products or services. Businesses blog to attract attention to their products and to establish themselves as experts, thus building trust and credibility. Ultimately, they blog to attract customers.

Blogging began as a personal, individual form of publication, and successful corporate blogs tend to preserve that sense of personality. Many of the most popular corporate blogs belong to very small businesses, where readers can get a sense of the individuals who run the business. Larger companies often run a group of blogs for different topics, and either assign writers to each blog or set up group blogs where employees take turns at writing.

I mentioned *Manolo's Shoe Blog* earlier in this chapter. Another fashion blogger is Thomas Mahon, a London tailor who specializes in handmade men's suits. In their early book on corporate blogging, *Naked Conversations*, Robert Scoble and Shel Israel described how Mahon expanded his business through blogging, carefully coached by the ex-advertising executive Hugh MacLeod. Mahon's blog, *English Cut*, which is still going strong, has no advertisements. In a sense, the entire blog is an advertisement. This blog is about connecting with potential customers and establishing Mahon as an expert in his field.

The first posts in *English Cut* explain the business. Mahon explains what a bespoke suit is, and the difference between such a suit and made-to-measure suits or off-the-rack suits. He shows photos of his workshop, of patterns being drafted and fabric being cut. He explains specialities of the different tailors on Savile Row, and tells us his prices. Later posts are then able to build upon this and frequently link back to these basics when appropriate. As Scoble and Israel note, 'Mahon, wisely, didn't try to sell suits on the new blog. Instead, he showed his knowledge and love of the craft. He explained the labor and why the cost was justified' (2006: 65). Posts on *English Cut* have included discussions of the qualities of various wools, an introduction to a new addition to the tailor's staff and a long, musing post about the care and time involved in crafts such as tailoring.

There are many reasons for companies to blog. In general, blogging is a way of communicating directly with customers without having to use the media as an intermediary. More specifically, blogs allow companies to establish themselves as experts in a field, to engage directly in ongoing conversations among their customers or to start their own conversations. Blogs are a way in which corporations try to create a 'human voice', as the authors of *The Cluetrain Manifesto* would have said.

Mahon succeeded in establishing himself as an expert in his field through his blog, explaining his craft using simple language and photographs. He even, in posts like 'If You Can't Afford Bespoke' (19 January 2005), gives advice on more reasonably priced suit purchases for people who can't afford his £2,000 suits. Posts like these give readers insight into a craft that for many had seemed completely inaccessible, and in this way he builds a much broader reputation for himself than would be possible using traditional means of advertising. He also keeps his existing customers engaged in the process while they wait for their suits to be completed (it takes about three months), for instance by explaining how they mark suits at a fitting, and how they make alterations based on these marks. Selling custom-made suits is a niche business – Mahon is never going to have millions of customers. Through blogging, though, Mahon has succeeded in expanding what used to be largely a local business, giving it global reach. As Scoble and Israel wrote, 'It's still a word-of-mouth business, but blogging has scaled it to global levels' (2006: 66).

Another reason that businesses might want to blog is in order to participate in the conversations about them already taking place online. Mike Torres, the lead program manager at the time for MSN Spaces, talked about this in an interview in *Naked Conversations*. Torres said he ran regular searches on Technorati for keywords related to MSN Spaces and, when he found bloggers discussing it, he would jump into the conversation. 'It stops the rants. A lot of times when you do that, there's a "Sorry – I didn't know you were listening" reply. One guy posted, "Big retraction: I was wrong." What happens is that if they know you're in the conversation, people get respectful. They may still criticise you, but they don't lie' (Scoble and Israel 2006: 20).

Many businesses have used similar strategies, as Google did in response to criticisms for having unfairly removed a website from their search engine. TalkOrigins.org was hacked by someone who added a hidden list of links to suspect link-farming sites in the source code in order to make the linked-to sites show up more prominently in search engines. The web-master didn't notice that this had happened, as the website still looked the same as before – but then he discovered that Google was no longer indexing his site. He could not find any information about *why* his site had been made invisible to anyone searching Google, but eventually found the hacked code and removed it. At 3 am on 3 December 2006, the webmaster wrote an angry blog post describing his dilemma on his blog Austringer.net. In particular, he complained that Google had not provided any information about what the problem was and that there was no way to contact Google to get this information.

At 11:21 pm the same day, Slashdot.org, a popular news site for technology, had picked up the story and posted it with the title 'Google De-indexes Talk.Origins, Won't Say Why'. *Slashdot* has been such a popular site over many years that being 'Slashdotted', or featured on *Slashdot*, has been known to crash a small website's server because it was not set up for the hordes of visitors coming from *Slashdot*. And Google noticed: less than three-and-a-half hours after the *Slashdot* post, Matt Cutts, head of the Webspam team at Google, blogged in response: 'If you've never read my blog before, welcome. I'm the head of the Webspam team at Google. And I have a blog for days just like this.' (*Mattcutts.com*, 4 December 2006). Cutts provided links to both the original post from *Talk.Origins'* webmaster, and to the *Slashdot* story. He went on to explain exactly how Google had handled the issues at *Talk.Origin*, and how they had tried to email the webmaster. He also apologized, saying that Google is working at doing a better job at this but he also affirmed that he believed Google already does a far better job than any other search engine.

Individual disgruntled customers can have a lot of power today through posting their complaints on their blog – or, even more damningly, by posting videos or audio recordings of bad customer service. A popular example is the video a customer posted to YouTube of a visiting Comcast technician asleep on the customer's couch, waiting on hold to speak to Comcast's repair office for assistance with the repair he was working on (Doorframe 2006). That video spread like wildfire, and also got attention from mainstream media (Belson 2006). Other consumers start fan blogs for brands they love, such as *Barq's*, a blog about *Barq's Root Beer* that is analysed both in Ben McConnell and Jackie Huba's *Citizen Marketers* (2007) and by Robert Kozinets (2006).

Mahon's blog is an example of the leader of a small business writing a blog profiling his company and himself. Cutts's blog is an example of a prominent person in a very large company writing a blog about his work. More and more large companies like Google are encouraging their employees to blog. Robert Scoble, who was a Microsoft employee when he and Shel Israel wrote *Naked Conversations* (2006), wrote enthusiastically about the large number of Microsoft employees who blog, even arguing that their blogging has shifted the general opinion of Microsoft from that of the 'evil empire' to a much more positive customer opinion (Scoble and Israel 2006: 10–11).

Big companies use blogs in different ways. Individual employees may run their own, personally branded sites that also discuss their jobs. Matt Cutts's blog does not have a google.com URL; instead, he blogs at *mattcutts.com*. However he clearly states that he works at Google, and most of his posts are in some way related to his job. Other companies set up group blogs where several employees take turns blogging. Or blogs can be set up about different topics, as at Arla, the largest Danish dairy, which has separate blogs for recipes, for environmental issues concerning milk production, for consumer issues, and, most creatively, for two farmers who supply milk to the dairy.

Some companies post guidelines for bloggers. Sometimes, these guidelines represent a total ban on blogging, as for members of the Australian military from December 2006 and of the British military from August 2007 (bbc.co.uk 2007), although these bans have since been lifted. In May 2007, the US army first issued what appeared to be a similar ban, and then, days later, loosened these restrictions, stating that 'In no way will every blog post/update a Soldier makes on his or her blog need to be monitored or first approved by an immediate supervisor' (Griffin 2007). However, blogs must be registered and will be spot-checked at certain intervals. More recently, soldiers have been warned against revealing their location online as this may be a security risk. While some soldier's blogs have disclosed poor conditions, others have been excellent advertising for the army – quite apart from the unique historical record created by these correspondences.

At the opposite extreme, we have Microsoft's policy on blogging as reported in *Naked Conversations* – at the time the book was written, they had no policy. That doesn't mean the legal department hadn't worried about it (Scoble and Israel 2006: 12) but, as Steve Ballmer says in an interview in *Naked Conversations*, 'We trust our people to represent our company. That's what they're paid to do. If they didn't want to be here, they wouldn't be here. So in a sense you don't run any more risk letting someone express themselves on a blog than you do letting them go out and see a customer on their own' (19). Of course, Microsoft's employees have chosen their jobs, and they can leave at any time. The latter is a luxury not afforded to most soldiers. After this interview, guidelines for 'Successful Blogging' were released at Microsoft, with a fairly simple list of rules, as reported by Debbie Weill at her blog *BlogWrite for CEOs* (25 January 2005). For instance, employees were asked to 'Respect existing confidentiality agreements', to 'Identify yourself', 'Speak for yourself' and 'Think about reactions before you post'.

The Walker Art Center is an example of a company that from an early stage provided liberal but clear guidelines for its bloggers, and in the interest of full disclosure and trust it has chosen to make its guidelines available to its readers as well (Walker Art Center 2006). In part, the guidelines simply remind bloggers not to break the law: 'Do not post material that is unlawful, abusive, defamatory, invasive of another's privacy, or obscene to a reasonable person.' There are also points that may be obvious to someone used to blogging but could be useful for newcomers: 'Get permission from colleagues before writing about them.' Some of the guidelines simply give basic advice on blogging style and etiquette, for instance asking bloggers to provide links when quoting sources.

Engaging bloggers

Micropatronage, sponsored posts and advertising on blogs are all ways in which individuals are able to set themselves up as independent writers who can make money from their writing. Most make very little, but some bloggers have succeeded in making a living from their blogs.

But from the point of view of the advertisers, these strategies are neither revolutionary nor necessarily particularly profitable. As J. D. Lasica writes, 'most of the marketing world has decided to take a different approach: Instead of paying bloggers or giving them fancy trips and freebies [what Annabel Candy described above as social media bartering: see p. 155], you establish relationships and engage those bloggers who care deeply about the industry that impacts you or your clients' (Lasica 2005). This is the approach taken by Stormhoek, a small South African winery that has become a prime example of a company that has successfully leveraged blogging – in the two years since they started blogging, their sales increased fivefold, an increase they attributed primarily to blogging, according to a post to Hugh MacLeod's blog *GapingVoid* on 29 December 2006. MacLeod is Stormhoek's blogging consultant. The same MacLeod was also the man who helped Thomas Mahon the tailor start his successful blog. In a video posted to the company blog, Stormhoek director Jason Korman says the following:

> With the incredible power of social software, why would you ever buy an ad? If you have something interesting to say online today, so many people will pick it up. A lot of what online marketing is about is having a mess of stuff out there so when people are interested in the brand, there are 1,000 things they can click on. (Davis 2006)

When Manolo links to other fashion blogs, he engages in conversations that are already occurring. The links are useful and entertaining to his readers, who thus find more blogs that interest them. Simultaneously, Manolo gains the goodwill of the bloggers he links to, who are then more likely to return the favour and link back to him – ultimately getting him more readers, which again leads to more money. When Thomas Mahon explains the origin of the phrase 'no strings attached' by showing us a piece of beautiful silk, just received from the cloth merchant, with little strings tied to its almost imperceptible flaws (*The English Cut*, 1 April 2005), he shares a small piece of knowledge packaged in a way that is easy for other bloggers to link to and share with their readers – thus gaining Mahon more readers for himself.

Stormhoek takes things a step further by giving readers tasks to solve. In August 2007, the winery promised a £5 voucher to the first five hundred readers to send in photos of themselves buying a bottle of Stormhoek wine. Running contests and promising consumers freebies is, of course, hardly a new marketing strategy, but the way this was presented on the Stormhoek blog was in strong contrast to the shiny image commonly projected by businesses: 'This might turn out to be quite groovy, it might not. Whatever. Fail fast, fail often etc. But it's a cool enough idea to make it worth a try' (7 June 2007). Stormhoek specifically doesn't want to look polished. As the director of Stormhoek said in the YouTube video, 'that sanitized, carefully produced life view wineries have tried to portray, people just aren't buying it anymore. Life just isn't like that' (Davis 2006).

Engaging bloggers by asking them to contribute is an effective strategy for bloggers who want to build a readership and a sense of community. It was used at about the same time by Darren Rowse at ProBlogger.com, who engaged readers by organizing a project called '31 Days to Building a Better Blog', where he posted daily tips on improving your blog, and additionally asked readers to post their own tips on their own blogs. If readers submitted their posts to ProBlogger.com by filling out a web-based form, Rowse promised to link back to their posts. There was no requirement that participants must link to ProBlogger.com.

Rowse achieved several things through this. It was a generous move, in that his coordination of the project gathered valuable information for bloggers trying to improve their blogs with the aim of making more money from them. He linked to participants, and as ProBlogger.com is highly ranked on Technorati and other search engines, links from the site are valuable. Bloggers receiving links will not only have new readers who have followed the link, they'll also gain a higher rating on search engines because they've been linked from an influential website. Of course, the project was clearly also to Rowse's own advantage. By activating readers, he gathered a valuable resource that was likely to attract many readers. Although he didn't require links from participants, most probably did link to him, which got him new readers and higher scores on search engines. By taking the lead in such a project, his status as an expert is augmented. And it gave him a clear agenda for what he will blog about for a whole month.

Sites like ProBlogger.com regularly post lists of tactics for getting more readers and readers that will return again and again. Such lists are in themselves very popular blog posts that gain a lot of attention from other bloggers. The business of making money by blogging is one of the most lucrative topics to blog on, it appears. Be that as it may, the advice given is clearly presented and well received, and applicable to those who wish to make money from their blogs, those who wish to establish themselves as experts, or those who simply enjoy the social aspects of blogging. The main advice is simply to engage with your readers. If readers leave comments, then respond yourself. Visit other blogs that are about the same topic as yours, and leave comments there – and link to interesting posts on their blogs. Some recommend more intense strategies, such as emailing new commenters and thanking them for reading your blog. Others have daily targets: visit five new blogs a day and leave comments on them, or make an effort to link to three new blogs each week.

The basic point is simple, though: blogs are a social form of writing, and don't work well in a vacuum. Some blogs can survive on transitory readers who simply arrive from a search – Darren Rowse's *Digital Photography Blog* was an example. A blog like this doesn't need to have a personal style or to establish relationships with other blogs because it is unlikely that many readers will return once their camera is bought. If they do return, it is entirely for the information given on the site. Many blogs want to build a brand, though, and in order to achieve that, you want readers to return again and again, and you want other websites to link to your blog in order to attract new readers. This requires engaging with your readers and with other bloggers, who often are your readers as well.

Corporate blogging gone wrong

People expect blogs to be honest and authentic. You can see that in Dooce's insistence that she will never allow her sponsors and advertisers to affect the content of her blog, and you can see it in bloggers' concerns about PayPerPost and the necessity of disclosure. When readers discover that bloggers they have been reading break with this expectation, the backlash can be enormous.

A Wal-Mart-sponsored blog that didn't disclose its sponsorship is a good example of a blog that didn't tell the entire truth. *Wal-Marting Across America* was a blog written by a couple who were driving an RV across the United States and staying overnight in Wal-Mart parking lots. The blog has since been deleted, with just a single post left to explain the story. The author, who calls herself simply Laura, writes that she and her husband had originally planned to do the trip as a vacation, and since she's a freelance writer, she wanted to write an article about it for an RV magazine. She asked Wal-Mart for permission in advance, and was thrilled when they offered to sponsor the couple if they blogged their trip. Unfortunately, Laura didn't disclose the sponsorship – and their blog was full of interviews with Wal-Mart employees who were unanimously happy with their jobs. Unsurprisingly, other bloggers failed to believe that the blog was authentic – it seemed too good to be true. Working conditions at Wal-Mart are such a contentious issue that anything that's so positive about the company is closely watched by organizations like Wal-Mart Watch.

The original blog posts have since been taken offline altogether, and removed from archive.org, but *Business Week* quotes a sample blog post, titled 'From Cashier to Manager': 'Now Felicia is a Project Manager for Corporate Strategy/ Sustainability and is very proud of Wal-Mart's efforts to protect the environment. . . . Wal-Mart is working toward an energy use goal of 100% renewable resources; targeting zero waste from packaging by 2025 and selling products that are good for the world' (Gogoi 2006). Richard Edelman, the CEO of the advertising company behind Working Families for Wal-Mart, the organization that sponsored the blog, was heavily criticized for the flop because he has often spoken out about the need for transparency and honesty in this kind of marketing. In fact, Edelman is a leading member of the Word of Mouth Marketing

Association (WOMMA), which has developed strict ethical guidelines that its members commit to following. There are even specific ethical principles for marketers to follow when contacting bloggers. At the top of the list of principles, it says: 'Consumers come first, honesty isn't optional, and deception is always exposed.' The *Wal-Marting Across America* debacle tends to confirm that.

The specific issue at stake in the case was the lack of disclosure: it was not made clear that Laura and her husband Jim's trip was fully sponsored and that they were being paid a salary in order to write the blog (Gogoi 2006). Jim and Laura were presented just as ordinary people with no special interests. This is specifically addressed in the WOMMA ethical guidelines in the section on 'Honesty of Identity', which states that 'Campaign organizers should monitor and enforce disclosure of identity. Manner of disclosure can be flexible, based on the context of the communication. Explicit disclosure is not required for an obviously fictional character, but would be required for an artificial identity or corporate representative that could be mistaken for an average consumer.' An obviously fictional character might be a character in a television drama or Barbie – yes, the doll – who also had her own blog for a while. Jim and Laura could, however, definitely be mistaken for average consumers rather than fictional or even sponsored characters.

In later interviews, Richard Edelman apologized for the dishonesty in the *Wal-Marting Across America* project. He also explained that the case had shown the importance of ethical training for all members of staff, as the people who had handled this particular case obviously hadn't followed the ethical guidelines that the company was committed to.

If nothing else, the *Wal-Marting Across America* blog and the resulting backlash show the importance of realizing that the ethical guidelines such as those put forward by WOMMA are necessary and an accurate estimate of most bloggers' and consumers' sense of justice.

Another way in which marketers have fallen into the trap of dishonesty is through apparent payola. Some companies have sent bloggers free gadgets – digital cameras, computers and the like – for review, much as they might do to the mainstream media. This has led to accusations against the bloggers who received these goodies and wrote about them. On *Slashdot*, the review copies of computers from Microsoft were seen as 'bribes' (27 December 2006), and in fact, some bloggers, like Brandon LeBlanc of *MSTechToday*, did write enthusiastically about the computer without disclosing that it had been a free gift from Microsoft. When found out, LeBlanc was viciously attacked by his readers, in comments to his posts of 23 December and 27 December 2006. Only a small number of commentators appeared to believe that he should have sent the computer back. What really irked readers was that LeBlanc hadn't told the whole truth from the beginning.

Nikon tried to avoid this problem in 2007 by sending fifty bloggers their latest and best model of digital camera, but on loan rather than as a free gift (or bribe, as some would argue). Bloggers who received the cameras had three options: send it back after six months; apply for a second six-month loan; or buy it at a discount, the money going to charity. One of the selected bloggers, Mack Collier, who writes the blog *The Viral Garden*, wrote that the reason he accepted Nikon's offer was their emphasis on honesty and transparency. He quoted the letter from Nikon in a post to his blog on 18 April 2007:

> There is only one requisite for receiving this camera: Should you decide to talk about your experience with the D80 we send you, in any forum, you must let people know that you got the camera on loan from Nikon. We want you to be as candid and transparent as possible about where you got this camera and what you're doing with it.

By emphasizing their desire for full disclosure and honesty, Nikon reassures bloggers that they are not trying to buy their souls or damage their integrity – and they additionally got good press from bloggers applauding their insistence on full disclosure.

Truth and integrity are at the core of both the success stories and failures of commercial blogging. Conventions for displaying truth and integrity have long been established in journalism, marketing and face-to-face communication. They are still in the process of being established in blogging. Although many mistakes have been made, conventions do exist, as evidenced by the WOMMA guidelines, the FTC guidelines and the similarity of outraged responses from blog readers when the basic trust is broken and a blog that has been presented as authentic turns out to be a marketing construction or fictional or heavily sponsored.

As *The Cluetrain Manifesto* asserted, honest conversation and the human voice are key to successful blogging. While this idea may have been neglected in the Gutenberg parenthesis of print and mass media, it is not by any means a new idea. As we discussed in chapter 2, Plato held that a dialogue with worthy listeners and the careful tending of communication is the best way to spread your ideas. If Plato were a marketing professional rather than a philosopher, we might imagine his being quite pleased with the way corporations are realigning their communication to a dialogue-based model.

CHAPTER SEVEN

The Future of Blogging

So will we still be blogging in twenty years' time? What about in fifty years' time, or a hundred? People like participating in the media. We like contributing and sharing our ideas, and we're unlikely to stop now that we have the technology to allow it. Participatory media that makes publishing available to everyone is like fire: once the cunning Prometheus had stolen the secret of fire from Zeus and given it to us mortals, there was no way for the gods to take it back. Countries such as Iran and China have tried to block blogging and social networks but citizens continue to find ways around the censorship. Iranians in particular insist on blogging, despite their government's attempts at suppressing it; in fact, by 2007, Farsi was one of the top ten languages used on blogs (Sifry 2007). With technology getting cheaper and easier to use, we're likely to continue to see shared media of all kinds – text, audio, still images and videos – and in more parts of the world between more groups of people. Participation in participatory media is still obviously limited by access to technology, to the internet and to the time and skills to use these. But more and more nations are participating. The ethnic and gender distribution of bloggers is also encouraging. In the United States in 2006, Pew Internet found that the ethnic distribution of bloggers was more balanced than that of the general internet population (Lenhart and Fox 2006). The distribution of men and women has also been fairly even (Herring et al. 2004; Lenhart and Fox 2006), particularly among younger age groups. This is promising for the future.

Blogging may not remain a separate activity or genre as it

is today. In the last few years, we've seen blogging spread into social network sites, and in some cases merge with them, as discussed in chapter 3. Karl Long of the blog *ExperienceCurve* described Facebook as nothing more than 'a blog template' in a post on 12 August 2007, and certainly Facebook incorporates many aspects of blogging: posts are ordered in reverse chronological order and there is an emphasis on the individual and the subjective. Facebook also automates many of the social networking functions that have been built around blogs. Where blogs use RSS feeds and trackbacks, Facebook simply includes all this in a single system. People blog on YouTube or Pinterest, with each entry a new short video or a link to a pretty picture. Perhaps we won't use the word 'blogging' in twenty years' time, but it seems likely that a form of personal publication, with links, social networking and brief posts, will remain.

Implicit participation and the perils of personalized media

When we talk about blogging, we usually think about the posts and comments that people write deliberately. But user-generated content is more than blog posts, images and videos. The most valuable information may be that which is implied rather than deliberately posted. For instance, you may not think of 'liking' a band or movie on Facebook, buying a book on Amazon, reading a news story while being logged into Facebook, retweeting something on Twitter or checking into a coffee shop on Foursquare as blogging or even really sharing information, but, taken together, data points like these form a picture of you that can be extraordinarily detailed.

This implicitly contributed information is data that can be mined for information that is more valuable than the individual contributions. Google uses the links between blogs and other websites as signs of peer recognition, mining the network of links in order to provide us with good search results. Other companies also mine data you barely consider that you've contributed: Amazon to give recommendations, Flickr to show the 'interestingness' of photos, and Facebook to show you the posts most likely to interest you. Political campaigns use 'microtargeting' to send personalized emails and show personalized ads to potential voters based on what they've bought, 'liked' and even websites they've visited. In a post to *O'Reilly Radar* on 15 June 2007, Tim O'Reilly argued that using this data is 'harnessing collective intelligence'. Collective intelligence doesn't lie in the individual videos on YouTube, or in each separate blog post we write; it's in the patterns we trace as we move through these media: the order in which we listen to songs, the books we buy after viewing a particular site, the links we make or the links we choose to follow.

We're still just beginning to mine these patterns for their data. In years to come, presumably the recommendations and understandings of what is valuable will be far more nuanced and sophisticated than they are today. Perhaps blogs, Facebook, YouTube and their ilk will simply take over and become the dominant media. Will conventional news organizations like the *New York Times* or the BBC or Reuters even exist ten years from now? Not according to the video *EPIC 2014*, an eight-minute Flash video created by Robin Sloan and Matt Thompson (2004) and presented as though told from the year 2014. The video begins by telling the story of participatory media up until 2004 – the invention of the Web, Amazon. com and its recommendation system, blogging, Google News and so on. But in 2005, the year after the video was actually made, history begins to change. Google buys Amazon, becoming Googlezon, and thereby merging Amazon's social filtering with Google's immense databases. Googlezon creates the Google Grid, which allows users to put all their life online. Microsoft launched its own competing systems. And by 2014, the way that we find and share information has changed. Here is a transcript of part of *EPIC 2014*'s voiceover:

On Sunday, March 9, 2014, Googlezon unleashes EPIC. Welcome to our world. The Evolving Personalized Information Construct is the system by which our sprawling, chaotic mediascape is filtered, ordered and delivered. Everyone contributes now, from blog entries to phone cam images to video reports to full investigations. Many people get paid too, a tiny cut of Google's immense advertising revenue proportional to the popularity of their contributions. EPIC produces a custom content package for each user, uses his choices – his consumption habits, his interests, his demographics, his social network – to shape the product.

This might not sound so bad. And it's not so far off, either. Google doesn't own the world to the extent that *EPIC 2014* suggests, of course; they share it with Facebook and Amazon and a few others. But they did, as noted in the video, buy Blogger.com. In 2006, they bought YouTube. For several years I have had a Google account that not only gives me email, it also knows which blogs I read and tells me when they're updated. It hosts my personal calendar, my to-do list and several of the documents and spreadsheets I'm working on. Long ago, I installed a Google toolbar that allows Google to track every single website I visit, giving me handy reports in return and helping me find those sites that I somehow lose though I'm sure I've seen them somewhere. Using this information, Google gives me personalized news. So far, the personalization doesn't seem very advanced. It knows to recommend news items about blogs, but apart from that it doesn't seem to know me as well as I would have expected, given all the data I constantly feed it. And clearly I'm giving up a lot of privacy for these services, as are other users who have signed up. More importantly, perhaps, Google also gives me (and you) personalized search results, meaning that when I search for something on Google I am not getting an objectively ordered list of results, but a list of sites that Google thinks I will like. As mentioned in chapter 3, this has been described as a 'filter bubble' (Pariser 2011) or an 'echo chamber' (Wallsten 2005).

Even if you haven't signed up for all of Google's services, Google knows a good deal about you. Google saves information about every single search, and connects information about search terms used and which links were followed to the IP number the search was performed from. IP numbers can tell you a lot about an individual. Some universities, for instance, have IP numbers that translate to exact locations, such as (these are made-up examples) dorm-room-231.univ-of-catalumbia.edu, student-pc-lab-23.humanities.ubilt.edu.au or even, sometimes, something like jillwalkerrettberg-room345.humanities.uib.no. Even when IP numbers are less revealing than this, they do announce your location, usually specifying the town you're in and your Internet Service Provider. If you're curious to see what your IP address is, go to a site like whatismyipaddress.com or search for 'what is my ip' and you'll find sites that will tell you, even placing you on a map.

But the customization that you get in return for the lost privacy can be extremely useful. I love it when Google finds news items for me that I'm actually interested in, or when Amazon recommends a book I wasn't aware of but realize I really want to read. Sometimes Facebook shows me posts from people I'm not friends with that have received 'likes' from my friends, and the posts often interest me: a photo of a colleague's new baby or a post from an angry Norwegian to Prime Minister Jens Stoltenberg's wall, for instance.

Used well, services such as the imagined *EPIC 2014* might be far more powerful than traditional newspapers and television. But they also give cause for concern. Here is another excerpt from the *EPIC 2014* video:

> At its best, edited for the savviest readers, EPIC is a summary of the world – deeper, broader and more nuanced than anything ever available before – but at its worst, and for too many, EPIC is merely a collection of trivia, much of it untrue, all of it narrow, shallow and sensational. But EPIC is what we wanted, it's what we chose. And its commercial success

preempted any discussion of media and democracy, or journalistic ethics.

That is why it's so important to know about what is happening,
and to think critically about what it might mean. In terms of
privacy, democracy and communication, blogging and social
networking sites are changing our culture. While we live in
democracies, do not oppose the government and abide by the
law, the loss of privacy doesn't matter to us. It matters greatly
in less democratic countries like China, where Yahoo! and
Google have given data about individuals' searches to the
government. It mattered to Hossein Derakhshan, a Canadian
citizen whose blog was searched by immigration officers when
he tried to enter the United States to go to a blogging conference. Derakhshan had spent a month in New York, staying at
a friend's house, and had written in his blog that he was cur-
rently living in New York. The immigration officer took that
literally – and as a Canadian citizen, Derakhshan had the right
to visit the USA for up to six months at a time, but not to take
residence there. Derakhshan was refused entry, but shared the
story in his blog, *Editor: Myself*, on 24 November 2005.

This problem goes beyond blogging, of course. It comes
with the internet, and with the ability to refind almost anything, even things that previously would have been forgotten
or at least not remained readily accessible. In *The Googlization
of Everything*, Siva Vaidhyanathan describes a case similar to
Hossein Derakhshan's, but where the immigration officer
found an academic article, not a blog post:

> Vancouver psychotherapist Andrew Feldmar [. . .] tried to
> cross into the United States to pick up a friend at the Seattle-
> Tocoma airport in April 2007. At the U.S. border, an agent
> decided to Google his name. The search yielded a link to an
> academic article Feldmar had published in 2001, in which
> he described his experiences with LSD while studying with
> R. D. Laing in the 1960s. Despite having no criminal record
> and throwing up no suspicious connections in government
> databases, the U.S. authorities barred him from entering the

United States because he had admitted using a controlled substance illegally. (Vaidhyanathan 2011)

Perhaps it is already too late to worry. We have, in a sense, already given up our privacy a long time ago. Margaret Atwood's book *The Handmaid's Tale* (1985) is set in a dystopic near-future North America where religious fundamentalism has led to extreme gender discrimination. Overnight, the government simply locks women's bank accounts so they cannot access their own money. Key cards to their workplaces stop working when the government decides that women should no longer have the right to work. During the Second World War, well before blogging or Google, the more detailed records a country kept of its population, the easier it was for Nazi invaders to persecute Jews and other groups. These acts of technologically assisted oppression were possible well before the internet, Google or blogging.

Blogs and participatory media have both a liberatory potential, as is visible in the energy of the Iranian and Chinese blogosphere, despite their governments' attempts to quash free speech, and a dangerous potential for increased surveillance and control. Blogs, knives and most other tools can be used for good or for evil. If we're aware of how to use them and of how they are being used, we can help to shape the future.

References

Abrams, M. H. 1993. *A Glossary of Literary Terms*, 6th edn. Fort Worth: Harcourt Brace.

acridrabbit et.al. 2001. Is it Possible that Kaycee Nicole Did Not Exist? *Metafilter*, 18 May. Available at http://www.metafilter.com/comments.mefi/7819, last accessed 16.4.2013.

Alerigi, Alberto. 2004. Brazil Internet Craze Angers English Speakers. *Yahoo! News*. 17 July. Was available at http://news.yahoo.com/news?tmpl=story&u=/nm/20040717/wr_nm/column_livewire_dc_1; use http://archive.org to access.

American Bureau of Labor Statistics. 2012. American Time Use Survey Summary. 22 June. USDL-12-1246. Available at www.bls.gov/news.release/atus.nro.htm, last accessed 18.4.2013.

Anderson, Chris. 2006. *The Long Tail: Why the Future of Business is Selling Less of More*. New York: Hyperion.

Andrejevic, Mark. 2011. Social Network Exploitation. In Zizi Papacharissi (ed.), *A Networked Self: Identity, Community, and Culture on Social Network Sites*. New York and London: Routledge.

Armstrong, Heather. 2009. *It Sucked and Then I Cried: How I Had a Baby, a Breakdown, and a Much Needed Margarita*. New York: Simon Spotlight Entertainment.

Atwood, Margaret. 1985. *The Handmaid's Tale*. Toronto: McClelland and Stewart.

Bahnisch, Mark. 2006. The Political Uses of Blogs. In A. Bruns and J. Jacobs (eds), *Uses of Blogs*. New York: Peter Lang.

Barabási, Albert-László. 2012. Network Science: Luck or Reason. *Nature*. Online, 12 September. Available at www.nature.com/nature/journal/vaop/ncurrent/full/nature11486.html, last accessed 16.4.2013.

Baran, Paul. 1964. On Distributed Communications Networks. *Communications, IEEE Transactions* 12(1): 1–9.

Barlow, Aaron J. 2008. *Blogging America: The New Public Sphere*. Westport, CT: Praeger.

Bastiansen, Henrik Grue and Dahl, Hans Fredrik. 2003. *Norsk medie-historie*. Oslo: Universitetsforlaget.

bbc.co.uk. 2007. Blogging Ban for the Armed Forces. BBC News. http://news.bbc.co.uk/1/hi/uk/6940120.stm, last accessed 16.4.2013.

Belson, Ken. 2006. Your Call Is Important to Us. Please Stay Awake. *New York Times*, 26 June. Available at www.nytimes.com/2006/06/26/technology/26comcast.html?ex=1187150400&en=84ddde3160f47559&ei=5070, last accessed 16.4.2013.

Benkler, Yochai. 2006. *The Wealth of Networks: How Social Production Transforms Markets and Freedom*. New Haven: Yale University Press.

Blogads. 2004. Reader Survey for Blog Advertising. Available at www.blogads.com/survey/blog_reader_survey.html, last accessed 16.4.2013.

Blood, Rebecca. 2000. Weblogs: A History and Perspective. *Rebecca's Pocket*. Available at www.rebeccablood.net/essays/weblog_history.html, last accessed 16.4.2013.

Boeder, Pieter. 2005. Habermas' Heritage: The Future of the Public Sphere in the Network Society. *First Monday* 10(9). Available at http://firstmonday.org/issues/issue10_9/boeder, last accessed 16.4.2013.

Bolter, Jay David. 1991. *Writing Space: The Computer, Hypertext and the History of Writing*. 1st edn. Hove: Lawrence Erlbaum.

boyd, danah. 2001. 'What's in a Name?' Available at www.danah.org/name.html, last accessed 16.4.2013.

boyd, danah. 2008. Why Youth ♥ Social Network Sites: The Role of Networked Publics in Teenage Social Life. In David Buckingham (ed.), *Youth, Identity, and Digital Media*. The John D. and Catherine I. MacArthur Foundation Series on Digital Media and Learning. Cambridge, MA: The MIT Press.

boyd, danah, and Heer, Jeffrey. 2006. Profiles as Conversations: Networked Identity Performance on Friendster. Paper read at Hawai'i International Conference on System Sciences, 4–7 January 2006, at Kauai, Hawai'i. Available at www.danah.org/papers/HICSS2006.pdf, last accessed 16.4.2013.

Brecht, Bertolt. 1964. The Radio as an Apparatus of Communication. In J. Willett (ed.), *Brecht on Theatre*. New York: Hill and Wang. Original edn 1932.

Brooks, Peter. 1984. *Reading for the Plot: Design and Intention in Narrative*. Cambridge, MA: Harvard University Press.

Brubaker, Jed, and Hayes, Gillian R. 2011. We Will Never Forget You [Online]: An Empirical Investigation of Post-Mortem MySpace

Comments. Paper read at ACM 2011 Conference on Computer Supported Cooperative Work, March 19–23, at Hangzhou, China.

Bruns, Axel. 2005. *Gatewatching: Collaborative Online News Production.* New York: Peter Lang.

Bruns, Axel and Highfield, Tim. 2012. Blogs, Twitter, and Breaking News: The Produsage of Citizen Journalism. In R. A. Lind (ed.), *Producing Theory: The Intersection of Audiences and Production in a Digital World.* New York: Peter Lang.

Burke, Carolyn. n.d. About Carolyn's Diary. *The Online Diary History Project.* Available at www.diaryhistoryproject.com/recollections/1995_01_03.html, last accessed 15.4.2013.

Bush, Vannevar. 1945. As We May Think. *Atlantic Monthly* 176(1): 85–110.

Canham, Matt. 2006. Utah Blogger Makes her Life Public Fodder. *The Salt Lake Tribune*, 14 October.

Cantril, Hadley, Gaudet, Hazel and Herzog, Herta. 1966. *The Invasion from Mars: A Study in the Psychology of Panic.* New York: Harper & Row. Originally published 1940.

Carr, Nicholas. 2010. *The Shallows: What the Internet is Doing to Our Brains.* New York: Norton.

Chandler, Daniel. 1996. Shaping and Being Shaped. *Computer-Mediated Communication Magazine* 3(2). Available at www.december.com/cmc/mag/1996/feb/chandler.html, last accessed 16.4.2013.

Chartier, Roger. 2001. The Practical Impact of Writing. In D. Finkelstein and A. McCleery (eds), *The Book History Reader.* London: Routledge.

CNNIC. 2011. 29th Statistical Report on Internet Development in China (January, 2012). China Internet Network Information Center. Available at www.apira.org/news.php?id=10, last accessed 16.4.2013.

Connell, Brandon. 2012. *Blogging for Income: The Fast Track Plan for High Traffic and Big Profits.* Self-published.

Cook, Trevor. 2006. Can Blogging Unspin PR? In Axel Bruns and Joanne Jacobs, *Uses of Blogs.* New York: Peter Lang.

Crisell, Andrew. 2002. *An Introductory History of British Broadcasting.* London: Routledge.

Davis, Lloyd. 2006. Marketing and Selling Stormhoek Wines. *YouTube.* Available at www.youtube.com/watch?v=ODvfb37nR_4, last accessed 16.4.2013.

Dean, Jodi. 2006. Blogging Theory. *Bad Subjects* 75. Available at http://bad.eserver.org/issues/2006/75/dean.htm, last accessed 16.4.2013.

Dean, Jodi. 2010. *Blog Theory: Feedback and Capture in the Circuits of Drive*. Cambridge: Polity Press.

De Maeyer, Juliette. 2010. Methods for Mapping Hyperlink Networks: Examining the Environment of Belgian News Websites. In *International Symposium on Online Journalism*. April 24–25, Austin, Texas. Available at http://online.journalism.utexas.edu/2010/papers/DeMaeyer10.pdf, last accessed 16.4.2013.

Doctorow, Cory. 2007. Scroogled. *Radar Online*. Available at http://craphound.com/scroogled.html, last accessed 29.4.2013.

Doorframe (pseud.). 2006. Comcast Technician Sleeping on my Couch. *YouTube*. Available at www.youtube.com/watch?v=CvVp7b5gzqU, last accessed 16.4.2013.

Dwyer, Jim. 2011. Four Nerds and a Cry to Arms Against Facebook. *New York Times*, 12 May. Available at http://www.nytimes.com/2010/05/12/nyregion/12about.html, last accessed 16.4.2013.

Eisenstein, Elizabeth. 1979. *The Printing Press as an Agent of Change: Communications and Cultural Transformations in Early-Modern Europe*. 2 vols. Vol. 1. Cambridge: Cambridge University Press.

Elatrash, Samer. 2007. Net Danger. *Montreal Mirror*. July 5.

el-Nawawy, Mohammed and Khamis, Sahar. 2011. Political Blogging and (Re)Envisioning the Virtual Public Sphere: Muslim – Christian Discourses in Two Egyptian Blogs. *The International Journal of Press/Politics* 16(2): 234–53.

Electronic Frontier Foundation. 2006. Apple v. Does. *Electronic Frontier Foundation*. Available at www.eff.org/Censorship/Apple_v_Does, last accessed 16.4.2013.

Epstein, Michael. 1997. Licence. In Horace Newcomb (ed.), *The Encyclopedia of Television*. Chicago: Fitzroy Dearborn Publishers. Also available at http://www.museum.tv/archives/etv, last accessed 16.4.2013.

Faris, Michael. 2007. *Traversing the City of Blogs: Pedagogy, Performance, and Public Spheres*. MA thesis, Oregon State University. Available at http://ir.library.oregonstate.edu/xmlui/handle/1957/6471?show=full, last accessed 16.4.2013.

Fort, Caleb. 2005. CIRT Blocks Access to Facebook.com. *Daily Lobo*, 12 October. Available at www.unm.edu/news/Oct05News/12cirt.htm, last accessed 16.4.2013.

Frey, Tara. 2009. *Blogging for Bliss: Crafting Your Own Online Journal: A Guide for Crafters, Artists & Creatives of All Kinds*. Asheville, NC: Lark Crafts.

Geitgey, Adam. 2001. The Kaycee Nicole (Swenson) FAQ Version 0.7. Rootnode.org. Available at http://books.google.co.uk/books

?id=MwJgMYt3JJMC&pg=PA89&lpg=PA89&dq=geitgey+The+
Kaycee+Nicole+(Swenson)&source=bl&ots=NlmKjUDBE8&sig=
Y57fiPZPtVuplWk66hRlRpkSzQ4&hl=en&sa=X&ei=CDx-Ucze
HLGw7Aa214G4CA&sqi=2&ved=oCDMQ6AEwAA#v=onepage
&q=geitgey%20The%20Kaycee%20Nicole%20(Swenson)&f=fal
se, last accessed 29.4.2013.

Gogoi, Pallavi. 2006. Wal-Mart's Jim and Laura: The Real Story. *Business Week*, 8 October. Available at www.businessweek.com/ stories/2006-10-09/wal-marts-jim-and-laura-the-real-storybusi nessweek-business-news-stock-market-and-financial-advice, last accessed 29.4.2013.

Granovetter, Mark. 1973. The Strength of Weak Ties. *The American Journal of Sociology* 78(6): 1360–80.

Greimas, Algirdas Julien. 1966. *Structural Semantics: An Attempt at a Method*. Lincoln: Nebraska University Press.

Griffin, Christopher. 2007. Internet Insecurity. *Armed Forces Journal*. Available at www.armedforcesjournal.com/2007/06/2740192, last accessed 16.4.2013.

Ha, Louisa and Fang, Ling. 2012. Internet Experience and Time Displacement of Traditional News Media Use: An Application of the Theory of the Niche. *Telematics and Informatics* 29(2): 177–86.

Habermas, Jürgen. 1991. *The Structural Transformation of the Public Sphere: An Inquiry into a Category of Bourgeois Society*. Cambridge, MA: MIT Press. Original edn 1962.

Habermas, Jürgen. 2006. Towards a United States of Europe. *Signandsight.com*. Available at www.signandsight.com/features/ 676.html, last accessed 16.4.2013.

Hall, Justin. 2004. *Justin's Links*. Available at http://links.net, last accessed 16.4.2013.

Hall, Justin. 2005. Darknight.mov. *Links.net*. Available at http://www. links.net/daze/05/01/pix/darknight.mov, last accessed 16.4.2013.

Heffernan, Virginia. 2006. 'Lonely Girl' (and Friends) Just Wanted Movie Deal. *New York Times*, 12 September. Available at www. nytimes.com/2006/09/12/technology/12cnd-lonely.html?hp&ex =1158120000&en=a56f0e777a707f56&ei=5094&partner=homep age, last accessed 16.4.2013.

Herring, Susan C., Kouper, Inna, Scheidt, Lois Ann and Wright, Elijah L. 2004. Women and Children Last: The Discursive Construction of Weblogs. In *Into the Blogosphere: Rhetoric, Community, and Culture of weblogs*, edited by L. Gurak, S. Antonijevic, L. Johnson, C. Ratliff and J. Reyman. Available at http://blog.lib.umn.edu/ blogosphere/women_and_children.html, last accessed 16.4.2013.

Hiler, John. 2002. The Date Project. *Microcontent News*, 30 October. Was available at http://www.microcontentnews.com/ entries/20021030-1892.htm; use http://archive.org to access.

Hooper, Clare and Rettberg, Jill Walker. 2011. Experiences with Geographical Collaborative Systems: Playfulness in Geosocial Networks and Geocaching. Please Enjoy Workshop at Mobile HCI 2011. Stockholm, Sweden. Available at http://eprints.soton. ac.uk/272471/, last accessed 16.4.2013.

Iser, Wolfgang. 1988. The Reading Process: A Phenomenological Approach. In David Lodge (ed.), *Modern Criticism and Theory: A Reader*. London: Longman.

Johnson, Steven. 2005. *Everything Bad is Good for You: How Today's Popular Culture is Actually Making Us Smarter*. New York: Riverhead Books.

Keren, Michael. 2006. *Blogosphere: The New Political Arena*. Plymouth: Lexington Books.

Khondker, Habibul Haque. 2011. Role of the New Media in the Arab Spring. *Globalizations* 8(5): 675–9. Available at www.tandfon line.com/doi/abs/10.1080/14747731.2011.621287, last accessed 16.4.2013.

Klein, Lambart. 2010. *Blogging for Pleasure and Money*. Self-published. Amazon Digital Editions.

Knights, Mark. 2005. *Representation and Misrepresentation in Later Stuart Britain: Partisanship and Political Culture*. Oxford: Oxford University Press.

Kozinets, Robert. 2006. Netnography 2.0. In Russell W. Belk (ed.), *Handbook of Qualitative Research Methods in Marketing*. Cheltenham: Edward Elgar Publishing.

Lanham, Richard A. 1993. *The Electronic Word: Democracy, Technology, and the Arts*. Chicago: University of Chicago Press.

Lasica, J. D. 2003. Blogs and Journalism Need Each Other. Available at www.nieman.harvard.edu/reports/03-3NRfall/V57N3.pdf, last accessed 29.4.2013.

Lasica, J. D. 2005. The Cost of Ethics: Influence Peddling in the Blogosphere. *USC Annenberg Online Journalism Review*. Available at www.ojr.org/ojr/stories/050217lasica, last accessed 16.4.2013.

Lejeune, Phillippe. 2001. How do Diaries End? *Biography* 24(1): 99–112.

Lenhart, Amanda and Fox, Susannah. 2006. Bloggers: A Portrait of the Internet's New Storytellers. Washington, DC: Pew Internet and American Life Project. Available at www.pewinternet.org/~/ media/Files/Reports/2006/PIP%20Bloggers%20Report%20 July%2019%202006.pdf.pdf, last accessed 29.4.2013.

Lessig, Lawrence. 2004. *Free Culture: How Big Media Uses Technology and the Law to Lock Down Culture and Control Creativity*. New York: Penguin.

Liebling, Abbott Joseph. 1960. Do You Belong in Journalism? *New Yorker*, 14 May: 105.

Lovink, Geert. 2007a. Blogging: The Nihilist Impulse. *Eurozine*. Available at www.eurozine.com/articles/2007-01-02-lovink-en. html, last accessed 16.4.2013.

Lovink, Geert. 2007b. *Zero Comments: Blogging and Critical Internet Culture*. New York: Taylor and Francis.

Matrullo, Tom. 2002. Loci Amoeni. *Commonplaces*, 21 January. Available at http://tom.weblogs.com/discuss/msgReader$786

McConnell, Ben and Huba, Jackie. 2007. *Citizen Marketers: When People are the Message*. Chicago: Kaplan Publishing.

McLuhan, Marshall. 1962. *The Gutenberg Galaxy: The Making of Typographical Man*. Toronto: University of Toronto Press.

McLuhan, Marshall. 1977. The Laws of the Media. *Et cetera* 34(2): 173–9.

Mead, Rebecca. 2006. Meg and Jason. *New Yorker*, 6 June. Available at www.newyorker.com/archive/2006/06/05/060605ta_talk_mead, last accessed 16.4.2013.

Milgram, Stanley. 1967. The Small World Problem. *Psychology Today* 1: 61–7.

Moglen, Eben. 2010. Freedom in the Cloud: Software Freedom, Privacy and Security for Web 2.0 and Cloud Computing. Presentation at Internet Society, New York Chapter, February 5. Video available at http://www.isoc-ny.org/?p=1338, last accessed 16.4.2013.

Mookerjee, Vijay and Dawande, Milind. 2007. In 2006, the Top 50K Blogs Generated $500M in Ad Revenue. University of Texas/ Chitika. Available at www.scribd.com/doc/219285/Blogging-Revenue-Study, last accessed 29.4.2013.

Moulthrop, Stuart. 1991. You Say You Want a Revolution? Hypertext and the Laws of Media. *Postmodern Culture* 1(3). Available at muse. jhu.edu/journals/postmodern_culture/v001/1.3moulthrop.html, last accessed 16.4.2013.

National Endowment for the Arts. 2004. Reading at Risk: A Survey of Literary Reading in America. Washington, DC. Available at www.nea.gov/news/news04/ReadingAtRisk.html, last accessed 16.4.2013.

Nelson, Theodore H. 1965. A File Structure for the Complex, the Changing, and the Indeterminate. *Association for Computing Machinery: Proc. 20th National Conference*, pp. 84–100.

Nelson, Theodore H. 1970. No More Teachers' Dirty Looks. *Computer Decisions* 9(8): 16–23.

Nelson, Theodore H. 1974. *Computer Lib/Dream Machine*. Self-published.

Nielsen, Jakob. 1997. How Users Read on the Web. *Useit.com: Alertbox*, 1 October. Available at www.useit.com/alertbox/9710a.html, last accessed 16.4.2013.

NM Incite. 2012. *The Social Marketer*, March 8. Available at http://nmincite.com/buzz-in-the-blogosphere-millions-more-bloggers-and-blog-readers/, last accessed 16.4.2013.

Notaro, Anna. 2006. The Lo(n)g Revolution: The Blogosphere as an Alternative Public Sphere? *Reconstruction* 6(4). Available at http://reconstruction.eserver.org/064/notaro.shtml, last accessed 16.4.2013.

NRK. 2011. TerrorTwitter. Available at http://nrk.no/terrortwitter/, last accessed 16.4.2013.

O'Baoill, Andrew. 2004. Weblogs and the Public Sphere. In L. Gurak, S. Antonijevic, L. Johnson, C. Ratliff and J. Reyman (eds), *Into the Blogosphere: Rhetoric, Community, and Culture of Weblogs*. University of Minnesota. http://blog.lib.umn.edu/blogosphere/weblogs_and_the_public_sphere.html, last accessed 29.4.2013.

Ong, Walter J. 1982. *Orality and Literacy: The Technologizing of the Word*. London: Routledge.

Pariser, Eli. 2011. *The Filter Bubble: What the Internet is Hiding from You*. New York: Penguin Press.

Peters, John Durham. 1999. *Speaking Into the Air: A History of the Idea of Communication*. Chicago: University of Chicago Press.

Pettitt, Tom. 2007. Before the Gutenberg Parenthesis: Elizabethan–American Compatibility. Plenary lecture given at Media in Transition 5: Creativity, Ownership and Collaboration in the Digital Age. Cambridge, MA: Massachusetts Institute of Technology, 27–29 April. Available at http://Web.mit.edu/comm-forum/mit5/papers/pettitt_plenary_gutenberg.pdf, last accessed 16.4.2013.

Plato. 1999. *Phaedrus*. Trans. Benjamin Jowett. Champaign, IL: Project Gutenberg. Orig. 360 BC. Available at www.gutenberg.org/etext/1636, last accessed 16.4.2013.

Poster, Mark. 1997. Cyberdemocracy: Internet and the Public Sphere. In D. Porter (ed.), *Internet Culture*. New York: Routledge.

Powazek, Derek. 2001. A Conversation with my Sister. *The Life and Times of Derek M. Powazek, Real Person*, 20 May. Available at www.powazek.com/zoom/log/archive/00000058.shtml, last accessed 16.4.2013.

Rainie, Lee. 2005. The State of Blogging. Washington DC: Internet and American Life Project. Available at http://pewinternet. org/Reports/2005/The-State-of-Blogging.aspx, last accessed 29.4.2013.

Rich, Cindy. 2007. Secret Life of Teens: Facebook – The Trouble with Facebook. *Washingtonian.com*, 1 August. Available at www. washingtonian.com/articles/education/4938.html, last accessed 15.4.2013.

Roberts, Hal. 2011. Mapping the US Popular Blogosphere. *Media Cloud*, 31 May. Available at www.mediacloud.org/blog/2011/05/31/map ping-the-u-s-popular-blogosphere/, last accessed 16.4.2013.

Robinett, Paul (a.k.a. Renetto). 2006. LonelyGirl15 is a FAKE . . . PLEASE WATCH!!! *YouTube* (no longer available).

Rowse, Darren. 2007. How Much Money Do Bloggers Earn Blogging? *ProBlogger*, 30 November. Available at www.problogger.net/ archives/2007/11/30/how-much-money-do-bloggers-earn-blog ging, last accessed 16.4.2013.

Rowse, Darren and Garrett, Chris. 2012. *ProBlogger: Secrets for Blogging Your Way to a Six-Figure Income*. 3rd edn. Indianapolis, IN: Wiley.

Ryan, Marie-Laure. 2005. Media and Narrative. In David Herman, Manfred Jahn and Marie-Laure Ryan (eds), *Routledge Encyclopedia of Narrative Theory*. London and New York: Routledge.

Scoble, Robert and Israel, Shel. 2006. *Naked Conversations: How Blogs are Changing the Way Businesses Talk with Customers*. Hoboken, NJ: Wiley.

Sennett, Richard. 1986. *The Fall of Public Man*. London: Faber and Faber.

Serfaty, Viviane. 2004. *The Mirror and the Veil: An Overview of American Online Diaries and Blogs*. Amsterdam: Amsterdam Monographs in American Studies.

Shirky, Clay. 2003. Power Laws, Weblogs, and Inequality. *Clay Shirky's Writings about the Internet* available at www.shirky.com/writ ings/herecomeseverybody/powerlaw_weblog.html, last accessed 29.4.2013.

Sifry, David. 2007. The State of the Live Web, April 2007. *Sifry's Alerts*. Available at http://www.sifry.com/alerts/archives/000493.html, last accessed 16.4.2013.

Skinner, Julia. 2011. Social Media and Revolution: The Arab Spring and the Occupy Movement as Seen through Three Information Studies Paradigms. *Sprouts: Working Papers on Information Systems* 11(169). Available at http://sprouts.aisnet.org/11-169, last accessed 16.4.2013.

Sloan, Robin and Thompson, Matt. 2004. *EPIC 2014*. Available at www. robinsloan.com/epic, last accessed 16.4.2013.

Thomas, Angela. 2006. Fictional Blogging. In A. Bruns and J. Jacobs (eds), *Uses of Blogs*. New York: Peter Lang.

Turnbull, Giles. 2001. The State of the Blog. Interview with Evan Williams. *Write the Web*. Available at http://writetheweb.com/Members/gilest/old/108

US Congress. 2005. House. Free Flow of Information Act of 2005. HR-3323. 109th Cong., 1st sess.

US Congress. 2006. House. Free Flow of Information Act of 2006. S. 2831. 109th Cong., 2nd sess.

Vaidhyanathan, Siva. 2011. *The Googlization of Everything (And Why We Should Worry)*. Berkeley: University of California Press.

Walker Art Center. 2006. Walker Blog Guidelines. *New Media Initiatives Blog*, 9 March. http://blogs.walkerart.org/newmedia/2006/03/09/walker-blog-guidelines/, last accessed 16.4.2013.

Walker, Jill. 2005. Weblog. In David Herman, Manfred Jahn and Marie-Laure Ryan (eds), *Routledge Encyclopedia of Narrative Theory*. London and New York: Routledge.

Wall, Melissa. 2005. 'Blogs of War': Weblogs as News. *Journalism* 6(2): 153–72.

Wallsten, Kevin. 2005. Political Blogs and the Bloggers Who Blog Them: Is the Political Blogosphere an Echo Chamber? Paper presented at the American Political Science Association Annual Meeting. Washington, DC, September 1–4. Available at www.journalism.wisc.edu/~dshah/blog-club/site/Wallsten.pdf, last accessed 29.4.2013.

Wardrip-Fruin, Noah. 2004. What Hypertext Is. *Proceedings of ACM Hypertext 2004*. Santa Cruz, CA, 9–13 August. Available at http://portal.acm.org/citation.cfm?doid=1012807.1012844, last accessed 16.4.2013.

Weinberger, David. 2002. Small Pieces Loosely Joined: A Unified Theory of the Web. Cambridge, MA: Perseus.

Wittig, Rob. 2003. Justin Hall and the Birth of the 'Blogs. *Electronic Book Review*. Available at www.electronicbookreview.com/thread/electropoetics/serial, last accessed 29.4.2013.

Woning, Randall van der. 2001. The End of the Whole Mess. Was available at http://bigwhiteguy.com/mess.shtml. Use archive.org.

Wright, Jeremy. 2005. *Blog Marketing: The Revolutionary New Method to Increase Sales, Growth, and Profits*. New York: McGraw-Hill.

Blogs Mentioned

A Little Pregnant. 2003–present. Julie. http://www.alittlepregnant.com
Apophenia. 1997–present. danah boyd. http://www.zephoria.org/
thoughts
Arla blogs. 2005–present. Maja Møller, Jacob Nørgård, Tove Færch,
Inge and Mikael Nørby Lassen. http://blogunivers.arla.dk
Barbie. 2002–2003. Mattel, Inc. http://www.myscene.com/barbie/
barbie_index.asp; no longer online; use http://archive.org to
access.
Barq's – the Blog with BITE! 2005–2007. http://thebarqsman.com
Boing Boing: A Directory of Wonderful Things. 2000–present. Mark
Frauenfelder, Cory Doctorow, Xeni Jardin, Joel Johnson, John
Battelle, David Pescovitz. http://boingboing.net
Brooklyn Tweed. 2005–present. Jared Flood. http://brooklyntweed.net/
blog/
Chronicles of Dr. Crazy. 2006. Dr. Crazy (pseud.). http://crazyphd.
blogspot.com
ClickNewz! 2006–present. Lynn Terry. http://www.clicknewz.com
Daily Kos. 2002–present. Markos Moulitsas (publisher/founder).
http://dailykos.com
Digital Photography Blog. 2004–2008. Darren Rowse. http://www.
livingroom.org.au/photolog
Dooce. 2001–present. Heather B. Armstrong. http://dooce.com
Editor: Myself. A Weblog on Iran, Technology and Pop Culture. 2002–
2007. Hossein Derakhshan. http://hoder.com/weblog
English Cut. 2005–present. Thomas Mahon. http://www.englishcut.
com
ExperienceCurve. 2003–present. Karl Long. http://experiencecurve.
com
Flowing Data. 2007–present. Nathan Yau. http://flowingdata.com
GapingVoid. 2004–present. Hugh MacLeod. http://gapingvoid.com
Get in the Hot Spot: Naked Travel Stories and Travel Tips. 2009–present.
Annabel Candy. http://www.getinthehotspot.com
Get Real. 2003–2006. Steve Boyd. http://getreal.corante.com

Get Rich Slowly. 2006–present. J.D. Roth. http://www.getrichslowly. org/blog

jill/txt. 2000–present. Jill Walker Rettberg. http://jilltxt.net

Justin's Links. 1994–present. Justin Hall. http://links.net.

Klastrup's Cataclysms. 2001–present. Lisbeth Klastrup. http://klastrup.dk

kottke.org. 1998–present. Jason Kottke. http://kottke.org

Kottke Komments. 2007–2009. http://kottkekomments.com

Kuro5hin. 1999–present. Rusty Foster (founder). http://www.kuro-5hin.org/

Links.net. 1994–present. Justin Hall. http://links.net

Lonelygirl15. 2006–2008. Miles Beckett, Ramesh Flinders et.al. http:// lonelygirl15.com

Manolo's Shoe Blog. 2004–present. Manolo (pseud.). http://shoeblogs. com

Matt Cutts: Gadgets, Google, and SEO. 2005–present. Matt Cutts. http:// www.mattcutts.com/blog

MegNut. 1999–present. Meg Hourihan. http://megnut.com until 2012, http://megnt.tumblr.com after 2012.

MegNut 2012–present. Meg Hourihan.

Metafilter. 1999–present. Matt Haughey (ed.). http://metafilter.com

Molly.com. 2003–present. Molly Holzschlag. http://molly.com

MotherTalkers. 2006–present. Amy, Elisa, Erika and Gloria. http:// mothertalkers.com

Mr Smash Goes to Washington. Mr Smash (pseud.). Blog previously titled *Citizen Smash, Lt. Smash, Indepundit*. 2003–2006. http:// lt-smash.com

MSTechToday. Unknown–2007. Brandon LeBlanc. http://mstechto-day.com [no longer active]

Narcissism, vanity, exhibitionism, ambition, vanity, vanity, vanity. 2001–present. Diane Greco. http://home.earthlink.net/~dianegreco until 2010, http://dianegreco.blogspot.com/ after 2010.

ntcoolfool. 2006–2010. Bryce Carter. http://ntcoolfool.livejournal.com

O'Reilly Radar. 2005–present. Tim O'Reilly et.al. http://radar.oreilly.com

Penelope Trunk. 2004–present. Penelope Trunk. http://blog.penelope trunk.com

PeterMe. 1998–present. Peter Merholz. http://peterme.com

ProBlogger. 2004–present. Darren Rowse. http://problogger.com

Quantified Self: Self Knowledge Through Numbers. 2008–present. Ernesto Ramirez, Alexandra Carmichael, Kevin Kelly, Gary Wolf, Marcia Seidler and David Masten. http://quantifiedself.com

Rebecca's Pocket. 1999–present. Rebecca Blood. http://www.rebecca-blood.net

Robot Wisdom. 1997–present. Jorn Barger. http://robotwisdom.com

Scripting News. 1997–present. Dave Winer. http://scripting.com

She's a Flight Risk. 2003–2006. Isabella K. (pseud.). http://shes.aflight risk.org; no longer online; use http://archive.org to access.

Slashdot. 1997–present. Rob 'Cmdr Taco' Malda, Jeff 'Hemos' Bates, Robin 'Roblimo' Miller (eds). http://slashdot.org

Stormhoek. 2005–2009. Hugh MacLeod et.al. http://stormhoek.com

Style Bytes. 2005–2008. Agathe Bjørnsdatter. http://stylebytes.net

Successful Blogging: For Small Business Owners and Writers. 2009–present. Annabel Candy. http://www.successfulblogging.com

Tales of a Bathroom Scale. Lori. 2002–2003. http://dietchick.blogspot. com

Tama Leaver dot Net. 2007–present. Tama Leaver. http://tamaleaver. net

TechCrunch. 2005–2007. Michael Arrington (ed.). http://techcrunch. com

techPresident. 2007–present. Micah Sifry and Joshua Levy (eds.). http:// techpresident.com

The Artful Parent. 2008–present. Jean Van't Hul. http://artfulparent. typepad.com

The Blogging Nurseryman. 2005–present. Trey Pitsenberger. http://the goldengecko.com/blog/

The Date Project. 2002. Anonymous. http://thedateproject.blogspot. com; URL since taken over by another blogger; use http://archive. org to access original blog.

The Dullest Blog in the World. 2003–2010. Anonymous. http://www. dullestblog.com

The English Cut. 2005–present. Thomas Mahon. http://www.english-cut.com

The Social Marketer. 2010–present. NM Incite. http://nmincite.com/ blog

The Quantum Pontiff. 2003–present. Dave Beacon. http://scienceblogs. com/pontiff until 2010. http://dabacon.org/pontiff/ after 2010.

The Viral Garden. 2005–present. Mark Collier. http://moblogsmopro blems.blogspot.com (this blog was recently made invitation only)

Wal-Marting Across America. 2006. Laura. http://walmartingacross america.com

We're in Debt. 2006–present. King and Queen of Debt (pseud.). http:// wereindebt.com

Where is Raed? 2003–2004. Salam Pax (pseud.). http://dear_raed. blogspot.com

Zen Habits. 2007–present. Leo Babauta. http://zenhabits.net

Index

Abrams, M.H. 31
advertising 135–6
  engaging bloggers 161–4
  exploitation and alienation
    152–5
  human voice in 136–9, 151,
    157, 168
  jobs 79
  micropatronage 145–6
  monetization 19
  sponsorship 139–44
  non-disclosure of 164–8
  and pay-to-post 147–52
  see also corporate blogs
Alexa.com 69–70, 142
alienation, exploitation and 152–5
Allbritton, Christopher 92,
    107–8, 145
Amazon 171–2
American Bureau of Labor
    Statistics 49
amplification/reinforcement of
    ideas 44
Andrejevic, Mark 153–4
anonymity
  bloggers 116–17
  journalistic sources 95, 96
Apple 95
Arab Spring 113
archives 72–3, 74, 84–5
  and narratives 121, 122
Armstrong, Heather B. (Dooce.
    com) 17–20, 23–4, 85,
    140–3, 146, 154, 155, 164–5
The Artful Parent (Jean Van't Hul)
    25–6, 28, 29

Atwood, Margaret 175
authenticity/credibility 97–101

bans/censorship 80–1, 113, 160,
    169
Barabási, Alberto László 70–1
Baran, Paul 69, 70
Barger, Jorn (*Robot Wisdom*) 8, 9,
    11, 12, 20
Benkler, Yochai 114
Berners-Lee, Tim 6, 56
Bjørnsdatter, Agathe 67–8
Blogads 97–8
Blogger.com 9–10, 11, 12, 33,
    141
blogging engines 5–6
  see also specific sites
'blogipelago' 29
'blogosphere' 29
blogs/weblogs
  definitions 30–5
  history of 6–14
  use and evolution of term 8,
    11, 12, 13
Blood, Rebecca 8, 9–10, 11, 12,
    128
BoingBoing.net 20–1, 70, 123
Borelius, Maria 111–12
boyd, danah 82–4
  and Heer, Jeffrey 83–4
Boyd, Steve 147
Brecht, Bertolt 57–8
Brooks, Peter 118, 124
Bruns, Alex 93, 108–10, 111, 112
  and Highfield, Tim 110–11
Burke, Carolyn 12

Bush, George W. 111
Bush, Vannevar 53–4, 56

Candy, Annabel 154–5
career advice 121, 122–3
Carr, Nicholas 49
censorship/bans 80–1, 113, 160,
    169
chance witnesses 104–7
China 113, 169, 174, 175
China Internet Network
    Information Center
    (CNNIC) 17
Chitika 140
Chronicles of Dr. Crazy 125–6,
    127–8
citizen journalism *see* journalism
ClickNewz! 151–2
Cluetrain Manifesto 136–8, 151,
    157, 168
co-construction: technology and
    culture 57
collaborative filtering 109
colliding networks 83–6
Collier, Mack 167
commercial blogs *see* advertising;
    corporate blogs
'communicative capitalism' 152–3
controversy, avoidance of 27–8
Cook, Trevor 138, 139
corporate blogs 155–60
    guidelines 160–1, 165–6, 168
    non-disclosure of sponsorship
    164–8
crafts blogs 25–6, 27, 28, 118, 123
credibility/authenticity 97–101
culture–technology interaction
    57–61
Cutts, Matt 158–9

The Daily Kos (Markos Moulitsas)
    24–5, 26, 27
data collection (texts) 43–4
data mining 170–1
The Date Project 116–17
Davis, Lloyd 162, 163

Dean, Jodi 29, 74, 152–3
deaths 126–7, 129
Derakhshan, Hossein 174
dialogue 38, 39, 40–1, 46, 168
diaries 7–8, 9, 12, 29–30, 125
    see also personal blogs
Diaspora* 82, 89
dieting blogs 117–18
Digg.com 109
Digital Photography Blog 143, 164
dissemination 40–1, 42–3, 53
distributed networks 69–72
Doctorow, Cory 81
Dooce.com (Heather B.
    Armstrong) 17–20, 23–4, 85,
    140–3, 146, 154, 155, 164–5
Dr. Crazy 125–6, 127–8
The Dullest Blog in the World 34–5
Dumas, Alexandre 46

ebook readers 119
Edelman, Richard 165–6
Eisenstein, Elizabeth 42, 43–4
Electronic Frontier Foundation
    95–6
emerging social networks 86–9
ending/quitting blogs 125–6
Engelbart, Doug 55, 56
English Cut (Thomas Mahon)
    156, 157, 159, 162
EPIC 2014 (video) 171–2, 173–4
episodic blogs, ongoing and
    118–27
ethical issues
    guidelines for corporate
    blogging 160–1, 165–6, 168
    implicit participation and
    personalization 170–5
    privacy 81–2
    sponsorship 164–8
exoskeleton for blogs 64–5
ExperienceCurve 170
exploitation and alienation 152–5

Facebook 11–12, 13–15, 16, 65, 141
    as 'blog template' 170

CNN partnership 51
as microblog 76–8
pressure to participate 80–1
privacy issues 81–2
Timeline 89
Virginia Tech shootings 105–6
visible and invisible audience
84
fakes/hoaxes 99, 129–34
fashion blogs 67–8, 156
Federal Trade Commission, US
150–1
filter blogs 20–3, 29–30, 92–3
Flattr 146
Foursquare 78, 86–7
Free Flow of Information Bill/
Act, US 96–7
freedom of the press 90, 91
freedom of speech 95, 96
Frey, Tara 28
Friendster 84
future perspective 169–75

garden blogs 151
gatewatching 93, 108–12
gender issues 28–30
goal-oriented narratives 116–18
Gogoi, Pallavi 165, 166
Google+ 85–6
Google 71–2, 75, 87, 170–3, 174–5
AdSense 141, 154, 155
Orkut 79–80
removal of websites from
158–9
Google Trends 63–4
Googlezon 171–2
Granovetter, Mark 66–7, 68
Greco, Diane 118
Griffin, Christopher 160
Gutenberg, Johannes 42, 86
Gutenberg parenthesis 47, 48

Habermas, Jürgen 50, 52–3
hacking 158
Hall, Justin (*Justin's Links*) 7–8,
12, 124, 126, 128

Herring, Susan C. et al. 28–30
Hiler, John 117
historical perspective
hypertext and computer lib
53–6
mainstream media 36–7, 100
modern public sphere 50–3
orality and literacy 37–41
social media 62–4
technology-culture interaction
57–61
weblogs 6–14
see also print
hoaxes/fakes 99, 129–34
Holzschlag, Molly E. 147, 154
Hourihan, Meg 21, 33, 120–1
human voice in advertising
136–9, 151, 157, 168
hypertext
and computer lib 53–6
definitions 54
HTML code 9

immigration control 174–5
inactive blogs 16
income 19, 94–5, 139–40
independent journalism 107–8
indexing/tracking 13, 16–17,
64–5, 69–70, 73, 87–8
internet
as distributed network
69–72
and freedom of the press 91
and public sphere 52
and television 49–50
intraskeleton for blogs 65
invisible audiences 82, 83, 84
IP numbers 75, 86, 87, 141, 173
Iran 169, 175
Iraq 92, 99, 100–3, 104, 107–8,
113, 145
IZEA 148–9

Jerz, Dennis 14
Jesus (Parable of the Sower)
40–1

job advertisements 79
Johnson, Steven 49
journalism 36
    and commercial blogging 139,
        147–8
    first-hand reports 101–3, 104–7
    gatewatching 93, 108–12
    independence and opinions
        107–8
    mainstream media 74, 90–3,
        97–8, 102–3, 105, 110–12,
        113–14
    objectivity, authenticity and
        credibility 97–101
    professional–amateur
        distinction: practical and
        legal issues 94–7
    self-perception 93–4
    types 92–3
Justin's Links (Justin Hall) 7–8,
    12, 124, 126, 128

Keren, Michael 103
Klastrup, Lisbeth 79
Knights, Mark 46, 52–3
Korman, Jason 162
Kottke, Jason (kottke.org) 20–4,
    120–1, 128, 145–6

Lanham, Richard 33–4
Lasica, J. D. 113, 148, 161
Lebanon 99, 100, 101
LeBlanc, Brandon 167
legal issues
    broadcasting 59–60
    professional–amateur
        journalism 93–7
Lejeune, Phillippe 125
Lenhart, Amanda and Fox,
    Susannah 29, 93–4, 108,
    139, 148, 169
Lessig, Lawrence 114
Levine, Rick 136
Liebling, Abbott Joseph 90
Lieutenant Smash 102–3, 104,
    106–7

LinkedIn 78–9, 82
links/linking 29
    see also social networks;
        tracking/indexing
literacy
    orality and 37–41
    'Reading at Risk' report
        48–9
    spread of 44–5
    writing 72
LiveJournal 14, 20, 29, 64, 104,
    105, 106
Living Colours 129
Ljungkvist, Magnus 111–12
location-based/geo-social media
    86–7
Locke, Chris 136
lonelygirl15 131–3
Long, Karl 170
'love' blog cluster 25
Lovink, Geert 97, 113–14

MacLeod, Hugh 156, 161–2
McElwee, Meg 123
McLuhan, Marshall 41–2,
    47
Mahon, Thomas (English Cut)
    156, 157, 159, 162
mainstream media 74, 90–3,
    97–8, 102–3, 105, 110–12,
    113–14
    history 36–7, 100
    legislation/regulation 59–60
    newspapers 46, 51, 113,
        122
    television 49–50, 50–1, 59
    see also radio
Manolo's Shoe Blog 143–4,
    162
marketing see advertising;
    corporate blogs
Marqui 147, 148, 154
Marx, Karl 153–4
Mead, Rebecca 120
MegNut 120
memex 53–4

Merholz, Peter 11, 12
Metafilter 10–12, 129
microblogs 76–82
micropatronage 145–6
Microsoft 159, 160–1, 167
Milgram, Stanley 67
Moglen, Eben 82
monetization 19
Mookerjee, Vijay and Dawande,
    Milind 140
Moulitsas, Markos (*The Daily
    Kos*) 24–5, 26, 27
Moulthrop, Stuart 56
MSN Spaces 157–8
MSTechToday 167

Narcissism, vanity . . . 118
narratives 115–16
    fakes/hoaxes 99, 129–34
    goal-oriented 116–18
    ongoing and episodic 118–27
    self-explorative 127–8
National Endowment for the
    Arts: 'Reading at Risk'
    report 48–9
Nelson, Ted 54–5, 56
newspapers 46, 51, 113, 122
Nicole, Kaycee 129, 130, 131,
    132–3
Nielsen, Jakob 119
Nikon 167–8
NM Incite 17
Ntcoolfool 104–5, 106–7

Ondrejka, Cory 72, 74
Ong, Walter 38, 39
ongoing narratives 118–27
online communities *see* social
    networks
Open Diary 9
Open Diary History Project 12
orality and literacy 37–41
O'Reilly, Tim 171
Orkut 79–80
Ortelius: *Theatrum orbis terrarum*
    43–4

pamphlets 45–6
Parable of the Sower 40–1
parodies 34–5
participation
    implicit, and perils of
        personalized media 170–5
    social pressure 80–1
Pax, Salam 99, 100, 101, 102–3,
    104, 106–7, 113
payola 148, 167
PayPerPost 148, 149–50, 151–2,
    164–5
persistence 72, 74, 82–3,
    84–5
personal blogs 17–20
    see also diaries
personal computers 55
personalization 170–5
Peters, John Durham 39–41
Pettitt, Tom 47–8
Pew Internet Research 24, 93–4,
    108, 169
photographs/photography 123,
    143
Pinterest 14, 16
Pitas 9–10
Pitsenberger, Trey 151
Plato 38, 39, 40, 41, 44, 49, 51–2,
    72, 168
Plazes.com 86–7
political blogs 24, 27, 92, 108
political campaigns 171
power law 70–2
preservation of texts 44
print
    -based mindset 60
    introduction of 41–4, 86
    Late Age of 47–50
    precedents of blogs 45–7
    and spread of literacy 44–5
privacy issues 81–2
Problogger.com 143, 163–4
pseudonyms 99, 127–8, 143–4
public sphere 50–3
publicly articulated relationships
    82–3

quitting/ending blogs 125–6

radio 50–1, 57–60
  War of the Worlds broadcast
    129–30, 131
Rather, Dan ('Rathergate') 111,
    112
'Reading at Risk' report 48–9
Rebecca's Pocket 128
reinforcement/amplification of
    ideas 44
reorganization of texts 43
replicability 82, 83
Roberts, Hal 26
Robinett, Paul 133
Robot Wisdom (Jorn Barger) 8, 9,
    11, 12, 20
Rowse, Darren 143, 163, 164
Ryan, Marie-Laure 32, 33

Scoble, Robert and Israel, Shel
    135, 156, 157–8, 159, 160
Scripting News (Dave Winer) 8–9,
    11, 12
search engines 152
searchability 82, 83
Searls, Doc 136
Second Life 72, 73
secondary orality 38, 39
self-documentation 88–9
self-explorative narratives 127–8
self-tracking 88
Sennett, Richard 50–1
Serfaty, Viviane 1, 20, 127, 128
Sew Liberated 123
Shakespeare, William 48, 60
She's a Flight Risk 117
'shield' laws, US 95, 96
Shirky, Clay 71
Slashdot.org 158, 167
Sloan, Robin and Thompson,
    Matt 171
'small world' experiments 67
smartphones 15, 58, 87
social media
  and blogs 14–17, 64–6

history of 62–4
  use of term 13, 63–4
  see also specific sites
'social media sponsorship' (SMS)
    149
social networks
  colliding 83–6
  development 62–4
  distributed 69–72
  emerging 86–9
  microblogs 76–82
  publicly articulated
    relationships 82–3
  technology 72–5
  theory 66–8
Socrates 38
soldiers' blogs 160
  Lieutenant Smash 102–3, 104,
    106–7
Soulemama (Amanda Soule)
    27–8, 29, 118, 123
spam blogs 16
spam filters 152
sponsorship *see under* advertising
standardization of texts 43
'State of the Blogosphere' report
    13
Stoke, Regine 126–7
Stormhoek 161–3
storytelling *see* narratives
students 80–1, 104–6
Sullivan, Andrew 153–4

TalkOrigins.org 158–9
technological determinism 57
technology
  and culture, interaction 57–61
  of social networks 72–5
Technorati 12–13, 26, 73, 75,
    149
television 49–50, 50–1, 59
Terry, Lynn 151–2
time issues 73–4
topic-driven blogs 23–30
Torres, Mike 157–8
Trackbacks 75

tracking/indexing 13, 16–17,
    64–5, 69–70, 73, 87–8
Trunk, Penelope 121–3
Tumblr 15, 99–100
Twitter 11–12, 13–15, 65, 74

US Congress 96–7

Vaidhyanathan, Siva 174–5
Van't Hul, Jean (*The Artful
    Parent*) 25–6, 28, 29
videos
    EPIC 2014 (video) 171–2
    see also YouTube
Virginia Tech shootings 77–8,
    104–6, 113

Wal-Mart 165–6
Wal-Marting Across America 165,
    166
Walker, Jill 32
Walker Art Center 161
Wall, Melissa 98, 100–1
war reports *see* Iraq; Lebanon
War of the Worlds radio broadcast
    129–30, 131
weak ties 66–7, 68

'Web 2.0' 63–4
weblogs *see* blogs/weblogs
website statistics 75
Weinberger, David 62, 84, 136
Welles, Orson 129, 131
Wikipedia 31–2
Williams, Evan 33, 34
Winer, Dave (*Scripting News*)
    8–9, 11, 12
Wittig, Rob 124
women bloggers 28–30
Word of Mouth Marketing
    Association (WOMMA)
    165–6, 168
Wordpress.com 5–6, 16, 64,
    65
World Internet Project 16
World of Warcraft 73
World Wide Web 6–7, 56, 75
writing 37, 38–9, 44, 49, 72

Xanadu 55–6

YouTube 14, 99, 101, 131–2, 133,
    159, 163, 172

Zappos.com 144